SELECT QUOTATIONS
on the
ART OF LIVING

Tom Lovett

Trenton, Georgia

Copyright © 2024 Tom Lovett

Print ISBN: 978-1-958892-25-1
Ebook ISBN: 979-8-88531-696-5

All rights reserved. No part of this publication may be reproduced, stored in a retrieval system, or transmitted in any form or by any means, electronic, mechanical, recording or otherwise, without the prior written permission of the author.

Published by BookLocker.com, Inc., Trenton, Georgia, U.S.A.

Library of Congress Cataloguing in Publication Data
Lovett, Tom
SELECT QUOTATIONS on the ART OF LIVING by Tom Lovett
Library of Congress Control Number: 2024903335

BookLocker.com, Inc.
2024

Table of Contents

The Author v

Introduction: Creating Beautiful Lives 1

Part I: Art In Daily Life.. 5

Chapter 1: The Art of Living 7
Chapter 2: Cultivating Artistic Skills In Our Basic Behavior............. 23
Chapter 3: Linking Art, Science, And Religion................................. 35
Chapter 4: Seeking Beauty, Truth, And Goodness 47
Chapter 5: Mystical Experience 65

Part II: Social Science 71

Chapter 6: The Need For A New Social Science................................ 73
Chapter 7: Beauty In Social Science 75

Conclusion: A Theory Of The Art Of Living 91

The Author

Tom Lovett is an independent researcher and a generalist. Many years ago, he became interested in three questions. Why do liberals and conservatives differ so consistently on such varied issues? Why do people fight so bitterly over political and religious issues? Don't our shared human interests outweigh our differences?

Lovett looked for answers in the natural sciences, in the social sciences, and in the humanities. Over time, he linked key knowledge from those sources into a theory of the art of living, a theory that honors our common interests. You can find it in his book *Creating Beautiful Lives* (2020). Quotations in this new book inspired him to complete that theory.

He has a BA degree in Political Science from Cornell College and an MBA degree from Northern Illinois University. His career in Wisconsin state government was in health care reform. He and wife, Anne, live in Madison, Wisconsin next to the University of Wisconsin Arboretum, a site of pioneering research in the science of restoration ecology. See www.tomlovett.net.

INTRODUCTION: CREATING BEAUTIFUL LIVES

In theory, we create beautiful lives by learning skills in the art of living. Most people naturally acquire some of these skills, but we can easily learn more. A great many eminent authors have written books on the art of living, and their books stimulate our everyday artistic creativity.

The quotations in this book illustrate the theory that artistry can become our way of life. These wise sayings come from a wide range of distinguished artists, scientists, religious leaders, mystics, educators, philosophers, and others. They are interesting all on their own, separate from the theory, but in this new context, they motivate us even more.

In the proposed theory, we modify our basic behavior with artistic skills. Like other animals, we create living space, obtain food, eat, court, have sex, parent, groom, play, build, form social bonds, fight, flee, and sleep. Doesn't everyone learn some skills while engaging in these behavior? Don't we sometimes learn artistic skills?

Science and religion can help us create beautiful lives. For example, they can lead us toward ancient ideals: beauty, truth, and good. Doesn't everyone experience those ideals on occasion? Can't science and religion be paths toward them in daily life?

In theory, the most important everyday art mediums are our own lives and our relationships with one another, with other species, and with nature. By modifying our behavior with artistic skill, we can release our highest human potential in beautiful, deep, moral relationships. Albert Einstein wrote, "The great moral teachers of humanity were, in a way, artistic geniuses in the art of living."

Part I's quotations demonstrate how...

- *Any area of life can become an art medium* (Chapter 1).

- *We can learn artistic skills in our basic behavior* (Chapter 2).

- *Many people link art, science, and religion* (Chapter 3).

- *Countless others urge us to seek beauty, truth, and goodness.* In theory, we seek them best through art, science, and religion (Chapter 4).

- *The ultimate mystical experience is profound unity.* We can experience that unity as we create beautiful lives (Chapter 5).

If we evaluate the proposed theory, and it works well enough, it will become scientific knowledge: a new social science. Part II's quotations show that...

- *Many scientists criticize the current state of social science.* Social science could help us more as we seek to release our highest potential and solve our social and ecological crises (Chapter 6).

- *Many social scientists focus on beauty.* Increasing that focus might lead to more scientific social science, perhaps eventually to a science of the art of living (Chapter 7).

In the proposed theory, beautiful lives are not uniform. The simple underlying patterns that exist in beautiful lives can be expressed in unlimited ways in our individual and social lives and in diverse cultures. How those patterns manifest depends on the socio-cultural environments that influence us; on our time, energy, and interests; and on choices we make.

Beautiful lives are not perfect. Imperfections, incompleteness, and impermanence exist in all lives. Our physical, mental, and other challenges do not limit the beauty that is possible in our lives. In fact, how we deal with those challenges and with the circumstances we find ourselves in is essential to our ability to radiate beauty. The trials of life provide opportunities for us to respond in beautiful ways.

The proposed theory contains language that might help us communicate as we create beautiful lives. A common language would immensely benefit countless people around the world who seek peace, harmony, and unity.

Author's Note: Some quotations include *he*, *him*, *his*, or *mankind*. In the past, those words often meant both male and female. Today, authors commonly use *gender-neutral language*.

PART I:
ART IN DAILY LIFE

CHAPTER 1:
THE ART OF LIVING

We are all sculptors and painters, and our material is our own flesh and blood and bones.
          HENRY DAVID THOREAU, *Walden*, 26

The whole of human life is filled with works of art of various kinds, from lullabies, jokes, mimicry, home decoration, clothing, utensils, to church services and solemn processions. All this is the activity of art.
          LEO TOLSTOY, *What Is Art?* 41

I tell you the more I think, the more I feel that there is nothing more truly artistic than to love people.
          VINCENT VAN GOGH, quoted in *If You Want to Write,* by Brenda Ueland, 172

[Philosophy is] the love of wisdom. It is the art of living a good life.
          EPICTETUS, *The Art of Living,* 84

As concerns the art of living, the material is your own life. No great thing is created suddenly. There must be time. Give your best and always be kind.
          EPICTETUS, *The Art of Living,* 113

Man alone, of all the creatures of earth, can change his own pattern. Man alone is the architect of his destiny.... You mold your character and your future by your thoughts and acts.
          WILFERD A. PETERSON, *The Art of Living*, 8–9

[Aesthetic experiences] can be generated by any situation. Some see beauty in a flower or sunset, some in a theatrical performance or a musical theme. But others see it in a person, as inner beauty, or in an act of courage or kindness. Others still see beauty in common objects and situations,... All these experiences resemble one another, just as people

in a family look like one another. We have the perception of harmony, of grace, or a magic appeal that is sometimes evident, sometimes secret.
PIERO FERRUCCI, *Beauty and the Soul*, 15–16

Every single act can be done with care or carelessly. Every single act can add to or detract from the sum total of beauty in our home and district. Those who fail to practice their creativity are not only impoverishing their own existence; they are losing one of the deepest springs of our future vitality and hope.
JOHN LANE, *Timeless Beauty*, 159

We can be creative in everything we undertake. Aesthetics, like praise, can have its beginnings in the simplest and most mundane aspects of our daily lives: the care with which we create a garden (see Chapter Six); prepare a meal and attend to the appearance of its servings; the mindfulness with which we arrange rooms and flowers; the attention with which we play and listen to music; and the care with which we practice our most intimate acts—coring an apple, cleaning a pair of shoes, making a bed, wrapping a present or playing tennis. Cooking, cleaning, sewing, knitting, making repairs, reading bed-time stories, writing letters, bringing up children; all of these can be practiced with— or without—imagination. And of course, in addition there is always the practice of the arts of music, painting, sculpture, writing poetry, film and theatre-making, and pottery. The art of living remains the greatest, most challenging of them all.
JOHN LANE, *Timeless Simplicity*, 84

[The arts of daily life] include the art of friendship, the art of making beauty where we dwell, the art of conversation, of massage, of laughter, of preparing food, of hospitality, of the sharing of ideas, of growing food and flowers, of singing songs, of making love, of telling stories, of uniting generations, of putting on skits, of satirizing human folly. The personal arts include the arts of listening and of healing, of enjoying oneself with others in simple ways; the art of creating our lifestyles and our communities; the art of conviviality; the art of parenting and of forgiving.
MATTHEW FOX, *The Coming of the Cosmic Christ*, 200

The healing arts are about ritual, art as meditation, community organizing, and community celebrations. These arts could assist any society in cutting its health care costs drastically; in putting people back to good work gardening, massaging, making music in neighborhoods, caring for the sick, assisting the handicapped in their own liberation, making lively the days of the aged ones (called "the treasured ones" by native peoples), caring for the very young, assisting single parents, healing the addicted to liberate themselves, teaching the illiterate to read and encouraging others to become educated, assisting young adults through rites of passage and in ways to respond to their call from the universe for work and relationship, and calling forth the healing of society's forgotten ones. Creation spirituality is all about the healing arts, and therefore, it is about putting people to good work again. Only a finite number of cars ought to be manufactured in this world, but when it comes to creativity—to healing and celebrating, to beauty and self-expression—the human species has an *infinite* number of possibilities.
MATTHEW FOX, *Creation* Spirituality, 110–11

Art in the true sense, I believe, is a way of becoming fully present in the real, a way for people to experience oneness with things and with one another.... Art is the characteristically human way of being in and loving the world. That is what I mean by "the art of living": the process of becoming absorbed into living, of becoming present in one's life. All of this is to say that art has a spiritual dimension.... art is human experience at its greatest intensity and greatest depth.... art is at its most authentic in the most modest and typical forms of human making. Craft, labor, play: such activities, which most people engage in daily, are the truest arts of our culture. My idea is that our enlightenment is to be found precisely where we already are; the idea is not to become artists or appreciators of art, but to realize that we are already artists and appreciators of art.
CRISPIN SARTWELL, *The Art of Living*, xi–xii

When we are listening to popular music on the way home from work, we are listening to art that is more typical of and more organically connected to our culture than anything in any museum. When we enjoy a well-designed and written advertisement, when we watch a baseball game on

television, when we raise our children with devoted care, when we work with absorption in our gardens, we are authentically experiencing art.
CRISPIN SARTWELL, *The Art of Living*, xii

[We] can dig our ditches, mow our lawns, shop for our groceries, or care for our children with devotion, with the feeling that these activities can be consecrated.... they can be experienced as artistic activities when they are experienced in devotion to process.
CRISPIN SARTWELL, *The Art of Living*, 32

The same charged spiritual atmosphere that fills a great work of art can fill a creativity class. In a sense, as we are creative beings, our lives become our work of art.
JULIA CAMERON, *The Artist's Way*, xvi

We hunger for what might be called creative living—an expanded sense of creativity in our business lives, in sharing with our children, our spouse, our friends.
JULIA CAMERON, *The Artist's Way*, 5

Art when really understood is the province of every human being. It is simply a question of doing things, anything, well. It is not an outside extra thing. When the artist is alive in any person, whatever his kind of work may be, he becomes an inventive, searching, daring, self-expressing creature. He becomes interesting to other people. He disturbs, upsets, enlightens, and he opens ways for a better understanding.
ROBERT HENRI, *The Art Spirit*, 11

But not only medicine, engineering, and painting are arts; *living itself is an art*—in fact, the most important and at the same time the most difficult and complex art to be practiced by man. Its object is not this or that specialized performance, but the performance of living, the process of developing into that which is potentially. In the art of living, *man is both the artist and the object of his art*; he is the sculptor and the marble; the physician and the patient.
ERICH FROMM, *Man for Himself*, 17–18

The artist, after all, is not just the major name on the artistic horizon—the composer whose paintings are promptly bought as they leave the studio, the poet whose next volume is eagerly awaited by public and critic alike. The term must cover anyone who tries to create something of himself and from himself. In fact, anyone concerned with heightening his perceptions or broadening the spectrum of sense—even if not externally productive—is certainly internally creative.
    IAN BAKER, "Character and Creativity," in *How Does It Feel?*, by Mick Csaky, 78

It is something to be able to paint a particular picture, or to carve a statue, and so to make a few objects beautiful; but it is far more glorious to carve and paint the very atmosphere and medium through which we look, which morally we can do. To affect the quality of the day, that is the highest of arts.
    HENRY DAVID THOREAU, *Walden*, 134

Before we can adorn our houses with beautiful objects the walls must be stripped, and our lives must be stripped, and beautiful housekeeping and beautiful living be laid for a foundation: now, a taste for the beautiful is most cultivated out of doors.
    HENRY DAVID THOREAU, *Walden*, 36

It is a great art to saunter.
    HENRY DAVID THROEAU, *Journals*, April 26, 1841

Each man is minimally the artist of himself. Each paints that masterpiece, or blotch.... Each man also composes the symphony of himself, or the dissonant noise he is, the song or the croak, concerto of affirmation, or mutter in his chosen dungeon. Each is the author of his own tale, as well—his saga, epic poem, vulgar joke, illiterate gabble. Each is his own scientist too.
    PHILIP WYLIE, *The Magic Animal*, 267

We've become narrow in the ways we think about creativity. We tend to think of creativity as rarefied: artists are creative, musicians are creative, so are poets and filmmakers. But the chef in her kitchen is showing creativity when she invents a variation on a recipe. A bricklayer shows

creativity when he devises a new way of laying bricks, or of doing the same job with fewer materials.
> TERESA AMABILE, quoted in *The Creative Spirit*, by Daniel Goleman, Paul Kaufman, and Michael Ray, 28

There is an old saying that life itself is the biggest art. I've felt that all the so-called arts are an apprenticeship preparation for behavior and relationship which is more inclusive, a wider orbit. I don't know who was ever the first to refer to the wholeness of our life and of the cosmic reality as being art. The clue is given in the word *art* itself. When we trace its origins as best we can, we find an old Indo-European syllable, *ar*, which meant "to fit together, to join." An example would be in the word *harmony* from the Greek word *harmos*, which means "shoulder where two bones are fitted together." The idea of art being the practice of finding connections, of fitting things together is very open ended.
> M. C. RICHARDS, *Opening Our Moral Eye*, 20–21

Every person is a special kind of artist and every activity is a special art. An artist creates out of the materials of the moment, never again to be duplicated. This is true of the painter, the musician, the dancer, the actor; the teacher; the scientist; the business man; the farmer—it is true of us all, whatever our work, that we are artists so long as we are alive to the concreteness of a moment and do not use it to some other purpose.
> M. C. RICHARDS, *Centering in Pottery, Poetry, and Person*, 40

Might not beauty, and the love of the beautiful, perhaps bring peace and harmony? Could it not carry us forward to new concepts of life's meaning? Would it not establish a fresh concept of culture? Would it not be a dove of peace between the various cultures of mankind?
> SOETSU YANAGI, *The Unknown Craftsman*, 104–5

The greatest art, while acknowledging the world's brokenness and our own flaws, conveys glimpses of a potential wholeness, in ourselves and in the world. One of our names for that tantalizing wholeness is beauty.
> SCOTT RUSSELL SANDERS, *The Way of Imagination*, 33

Art of Living

There are three words that convey the secret of the art of living, the secret of all success and happiness: One With Life.
> ECKHART TOLLE, *A New Earth*, 115

Slavery was indeed the sum of all villainies, the cause of all sorrow, the root of all prejudice; Emancipation was the key to a promised land of sweeter beauty.
> W. E. B. DU BOIS, *The Souls of Black Folk*, 4

[Under slavery] the exquisite native appreciation of the beautiful became an infinite capacity for dumb suffering.
> W. E. B. DU BOIS, *The Souls of Black Folk*, 121

Surely there shall yet dawn some mighty morning... when men ask of the workman, not, "Is he white?" but "Can he work?" When men ask artists, not "Are they black?" but "Do they know?"
> W. E. B. DU BOIS, *The Souls of Black Folk*, 130–31

All the arts (as you have learned from this book) have but one single purpose, to contribute to the art of living and therefore they are closely related to each other and support each other and help each other out, like the members of a well-balanced family.
> HENDRIK WILLEM VAN LOON, *The Arts*, 635

We live in succession, in division, in parts, in particles. Meantime within man is the soul of the whole; the wise silence; the universal beauty, to which every part and particle is equally related,... We see the world piece by piece, as the sun, the moon, the animal, the tree; but the whole of which these are the shining parts, is the soul.
> RALPH WALDO EMERSON, *Essential Writings of Ralph Waldo Emerson*, 237

He has loved not only human beauty but everything beautiful in general: a beautiful horse, a beautiful dog, a beautiful landscape, a beautiful mountain, a beautiful forest, and every place and thing which is beautiful and rare of its kind, admiring them all with marveling love and selecting

beauty from nature as the bees gather honey from flowers, to use it later in his works.
ASCANIO CONDIVI, *Life of Michelangelo*, 167

Everybody needs beauty as well as bread, places to play in and pray in, where Nature may heal and cheer and give strength to body and soul.
JOHN MUIR, *The Yosemite*, 192

Heaven knows that John [the] Baptist was not more eager to get all his fellow sinners into the Jordan than I to baptize all of mine in the beauty of God's mountains.
JOHN MUIR, *John of the Mountains*, 86

The whole body seems to feel beauty when exposed to it as it feels the campfire or sunshine, entering, not by the eyes alone, but equally through all one's flesh like radiant heat, making a passionate ecstatic pleasure-glow not explainable.
JOHN MUIR, *John Muir: Spiritual Writings*, 65

The human mind and body are precisely adapted to this world, notwithstanding its trials and dangers, and that is why we think it is beautiful. In this respect *Homo sapiens* conforms to a basic principle of organic evolution, that all species prefer and gravitate to the environment in which their genes were assembled. It is called "habitat selection." There lies survival for humanity, and there lies mental peace, as prescribed by our genes. We are consequently unlikely ever to find any other place or conceive of any other home as beautiful as this blue planet was before we began to change it.
E. O. WILSON, *Consilience: The Unity of Knowledge*, 278

Once we recognize that art is intrinsic to our specieshood—to our *humanity*—each of us should feel permission and justification for taking the trouble to live our life with care and thought for its quality.... [Art is] a fundamental behavioral characteristic that demands and deserves to be promoted and nourished. Artlike activities exist in all societies and all walks of life. What is far more timely and relevant than its intrinsic sanctity or freedom should be the awareness that art, as the universal human predilection to make important things special, deserves support and cultivation—in schools, communities, and indeed the lives of everyone, not just artists in an artworld.

         ELLEN DISSANAYAKE, *Homo Aestheticus*, 225

There is already much to indicate a close relationship between esthetics and selective advantage, between beauty and viability, between the arts and life.... art constitutes what is close to being a single and profound perspective on our many cultures, focusing on issues that we deem to be of the greatest interest.... art constitutes the most comprehensive index of our common heritage, our deepest point of access into what may turn out to be our shared human nature.

      BRETT COOKE and FREDERICK TURNER, *Biopoetics*, 4–5

All human societies possess the concept of beauty, often with a very precise vocabulary and a tradition of argument about it. People see (hear, touch, taste, and smell) the beautiful, and recognize it by a natural intuition and a natural pleasure.... our capacity to perceive and create beauty is a characteristic of an animal that evolved.

         FREDERICK TURNER, *Rebirth of Value*, 4–5

If we look at humanity as a whole, we are social animals. Moreover, the structures of the modern economy, education, and so on, illustrate that the world has become a smaller place and that we depend heavily on one another. Under such circumstances, I think the only option is to live and work together harmoniously, and keep in our minds the interest of the whole of humanity. That is the only outlook and way we must adopt for our survival. By nature, especially as a human being, my interests are not independent of others. My happiness depends on others' happiness.

     HIS HOLINESS THE DALAI LAMA, *The Art of Living*, 107

A healthy sense of beauty is one of the key factors in the passion for work that dissolves the work/leisure dichotomy. To see beauty in professional experience is to build an important connection between our "public" and "private" selves, between the rational tasks we perform and our latent psychic energies.

      ROBERT GRUDIN, *The Grace of Great Things*, 14

The recalling of beautiful things, whether they are your own experiences or the achievements of others, is a creative act. Simple ideas can be restated by rote; but profound ideas must be recreated by will and imagination.
ROBERT GRUDIN, *Time and the Art of Living*, 183

The survival of our whole civilization may depend on whether we... experience the wholeness of nature and the art of living with it in harmony.
FRITJOF CAPRA, *The Tao of Physics*, 307

The goal of life is rapture. Art is the way we experience it.
JOSEPH CAMPBELL, *Reflections on the Art of Living*, edited by Diane Osbon, 247

People should be beautiful in every way—in their faces, in the way they dress, in their thoughts, and in their innermost selves.
ANTON CHEKHOV, *Familiar Quotations*, John Bartlett, 695

Her own personality was, in its way, a considerable work of art, expressing alike in her conversation, her dress, and the decoration of her houses, a fantastic individual and creative imagination.
LORD DAVID CECIL, on Lady Morrell, quoted by Paul Johnson in *Heroes*, 203

Every human being is an artist.
JOSEPH BEUYS, quoted in *How Does It Feel?* edited by Mick Csaky, 140

This is what it is to be human: to learn and assimilate the patterns of culture, community, and environment, both conscious and unconscious, and alter them as needed, make them ours, so that the voice spontaneously emerging is our voice, interdependent with the human world in which we live. Thus we breathe life into art and art into life.
STEPHEN NACHMANOVITCH, *The Art of Is*, 2

We can then say, with the Balinese, we have no art. Everything we do is art.
STEPHEN NACHMANOVITCH, *Free Play*, 19

My life itself became a work of art. I had found a voice. I was whole again. The experience was very much like what we read of in connection with the lives of Zen initiates.
> HENRY MILLER, "Reflections on Writing," in *Wisdom of the Heart*, 21

The wisest and most recognizably greatest practical philosophers of both these lands [China, Greece] have believed that the whole of life, even government, is an art of definitely like kind with the other arts, such as that of music or the dance.
> HAVELOCK ELLIS, *The Dance of Life*, 3

In ordinary life, creativity means making something for the soul out of every experience.
> THOMAS MOORE, *Care of the Soul*, 198

As we do our daily work, make our homes and marriages, raise our children, and fabricate a culture, we are all being creative. Entering our fate with generous attentiveness and care, we enjoy a soulful kind of creativity that may or may not have the brilliance of the work of great artists.
> THOMAS MOORE, *Care of the Soul*, 199

All work is sacred, whether you are building a road, cutting a person's hair, or taking out the garbage.
> THOMAS MOORE, *Care of the Soul*, 182

Many of the arts practiced at home are especially nourishing to the soul because they foster contemplation and demand a degree of artfulness, such as arranging flowers, cooking, making repairs.
> THOMAS MOORE, *Care of the Soul*, 288

The example of artists teaches us that every day we can transform ordinary experiences into the material of soul—in diaries, poems, drawings, music, letters, watercolors.... Our great museums of art are simply a grand model for the more modest museum that is our home.
> THOMAS MOORE, *Care of the Soul*, 301

Don't narrow your definition of an artist to professional painters, sculptors, musicians, or writers. You can apply the creative problem-solving skills you gained from this book to any field, be it medicine, psychology, science, economics, technology, architecture, or clothing design. You can even use it to enrich and re-create your relationships.
JUDITH CORNELL, *Drawing the Light from Within*, 196

If we can see that we are mutually dependent upon one another and upon that mosaic of natural and human neighborhoods we call "the world," then it should not be too hard to see that there ought to be responsible connections between science and the knowledge of how to live, and between art and the art of living, and that there is always, inescapably, acknowledged or not, a complex connection between art and science.
WENDELL BERRY, *Life Is a Miracle*, 89

For much of human history, the art of the hero wasn't left up to chance; it was a multidisciplinary endeavor devoted to optimal nutrition, physical self-mastery, and mental conditioning. The hero's skills were studied, practiced, and perfected, then passed along from parent to child and teacher to student. The art of the hero wasn't about being brave; it was about being so competent that bravery wasn't an issue.
CHRISTOPHER MCDOUGALL, *Natural Born Heroes*, 12–13

We need to be surrounded as much as possible with beauty. If we had this as the goal of our society, we could turn the world into a paradise that would be beautiful to both the eye and the mind.
WILLIAM COPERTHWAITE, *A Handmade Life*, 22

Japanese arts share certain aesthetics; and more important, they demand that acquisition of related positive character traits for their successful performance. Notice that many of the names for these arts end in the Japanese word *Do*. *Do* means "the Way," and its use in these names indicates that an activity has surpassed its utilitarian purpose and been raised to the level of art, that its students are practicing it as a Way of life.... It is absolutely true that practicing one of the Ways can lead to an understanding of the art of living life itself.
H. E. DAVEY, *Living the Japanese Arts and Ways*, 10–11

It is quite impossible to consider the building as one thing, its furnishings another and setting and environment still another. The Spirit in which these buildings are conceived sees all these together as one thing.... The very chairs and tables, cabinets and even musical instruments, where practicable, are of the building itself, never fixtures upon it.
    FRANK LLOYD WRIGHT, quoted in *Frank Lloyd Wright: In the Realm of Ideas*, edited by Bruce Brooks Pfeiffer and Gerald Nordland, 140

His [Frank Lloyd Wright] interest in every detail of building knew no boundaries.... After the basic grammar of form and structure must come the detailed items for use and delight, carrying out the same theme with color, texture, contrasts of dark and light, and changes of scale. This involved loving concern for design and harmonious relationships of all furniture, lighting, carpets, textiles, "stained" glass, sculptured or other integral ornamentation, and at times such accessories as china, silverware, and flower vases.
    AARON GREEN, quoted in *Frank Lloyd Wright; In The Realm of Ideas*, edited by Bruce Brooks Pfeiffer and Gerald Nordland, 140

Her [Japan] civilization became a true work of Art. No more valuable object lesson was ever afforded civilization than this instance of a people who have made of their land and the buildings upon it, of their gardens, their manners and garb, their utensils, adornments, and their very gods, a single consistent whole, inspired by a living sympathy with Nature as spontaneous as it was inevitable.
    FRANK LLOYD WRIGHT, *Frank Lloyd Wright Collected Writings*, vol. 1, edited by Bruce Brooks Pfeiffer, 119

Art ties us together with filaments of imagination and entangles us more deeply in our humanity. It inscribes our space, inward and outward, with the transformations of life. it is our fusion with the world by means of our fusion with one another, and our fusion with one another by means of our fusion with the world. It is sensual, abstract, immediate, distant, clear and enigmatic.
    BEN-AMI SCHARFSTEIN, *Of Birds, Beasts, and Other Artists: An Essay on the Universality of Art*, 230

It seems to me that the various esthetic concepts or attitudes that I have just finished describing—the Neoplatonic or otherwise mystical ones of Europe; the fertility-seeking, community-binding dynamism of Africa; the dramatic art leading to the rapt identification and releasing equanimity of India; the interlocking vital forces of China; and the indescribable overtones of Japan—all have something in common, common and important enough to be grasped as the esthetic universal. The universal is related to the modern German concept of *Enfuhlung*, translated by the English neologism *empathy*, whose mystical sources are in Herder, Novalis, and others. Empathy, however, is less than mystical, for it is simply the outward projection of one's consciousness causing other persons or objects to be experienced as if oneself.

    BEN-AMI SCHARFSTEIN, *Of Birds, Beasts, and Other Artists*, 226

In the last years of her life, my grandmother often woke up hearing in her mind the words from her beloved Dostoyevsky: "The world will be saved by beauty." Of all the words she wrote, of all the quotes she loved to repeat, of all the advice and comfort she gave to countless people, in all five of her books and fifty years of her column, and in a life-time of diary- and letter-writing, this is what has come to give me the most hope. For if, after years of struggle, weariness, and a sense of deep and abiding failure, she believed in salvation through beauty, then how can we not listen?

    KATE HENNESSY, *Dorothy Day: The World Will Be Saved by Beauty*, ix

A primary task is thus imposed upon one who undertakes to write upon the philosophy of the fine arts. This task is to restore continuity between the refined and intensified forms of experience that are works of art and the everyday events, doings, and sufferings that are universally recognized to constitute experience.

    JOHN DEWEY, *Art as Experience*, 3

We do not have to travel to the ends of the earth nor return many millennia in time to find peoples for whom everything that intensifies the sense of immediate living is an object of intense admiration.... Domestic utensils, furnishings of tent and house, rugs, mats, jars, pots, bows, spears, were wrought with such delighted care that today we hunt them out and give them places of honor in our art museums.

JOHN DEWEY, *Art as Experience*, 6

A conception of fine art that sets out from its connection with discovered qualities of ordinary experience will be able to indicate the factors and forces that favor the normal development of common human activities into matters of artistic value.

JOHN DEWEY, *Art as Experience*, 11

It is this degree of completeness of living in the experience of making and of perceiving that makes the difference between what is fine or esthetic in art and what is not.

JOHN DEWEY, *Art as Experience*, 26

Man is a thinking reed but his great works are done when he is not calculating and thinking. "Childlikeness" has to be restored with long years of training in the art of self-forgetfulness. When this is attained, man thinks yet he does not think. He thinks like the showers coming down from the sky; he thinks like the waves rolling on the ocean; he thinks like the stars illuminating the nightly heavens; he thinks like the green foliage shooting forth in the relaxing spring breeze. Indeed, he is the showers, the ocean, the stars, the foliage. When a man reaches this stage of "spiritual" development, he is a Zen artist of life. He does not need, like the painter, a canvas, brushes, and paints; nor does he require, like the archer, the bow and arrow and target, and other paraphernalia. He has his limbs, body, head, and other parts. His Zen-life expresses itself by means of all these "tools" which are important to its manifestation. His hands and feet are the brushes and the whole universe is the canvas on which he depicts his life for seventy, eighty, or even ninety years. This picture is "history."

DAISETZ SUZUKI, in *Zen in the Art of Archery* by Eugen Herrigel, vii–viii

One of the first requisites of a tea-master is the knowledge of how to sweep, clean, and wash, for there is an art in cleaning and dusting.

KAKUZO OKAKURA, *The Book of Tea*, 68

The tea-master held that real appreciation of art is only possible to those who make of it a living influence. Thus they sought to regulate their daily life by the high standard of refinement which obtained in the tea-room. In all circumstances serenity of mind should be maintained, and conversation should be so conducted as never to mar the harmony of the surroundings. The cut and color of the dress, the poise of the body, and the manner of walking could all be made expressions of artistic personality. These were matters not to be lightly ignored, for until one has made himself beautiful he has no right to approach beauty. Thus the tea master strove to be more than the artist—art itself. It was the Zen of aestheticism.

KAKUZO OKAKURA, *The Book of Tea*, 87

Great as has been the influence of the tea-masters in the field of art, it is as nothing compared to that which they have exerted on the conduct of life. Not only in the usages of polite society, but also in the arrangement of all our domestic details, do we feel the presence of the tea-masters. Many of our delicate dishes, as well as our way of serving food, are their inventions. They have taught us to dress only in garments of sober colors. They have instructed us in the proper spirit in which to approach flowers. They have given emphasis to our natural love of simplicity, and shown us the beauty of humility.

KAKUZO OKAKURA, *The Book of Tea*, 88

Tea with us became more than an idealisation of the form of drinking; it is a religion of the art of life.

BRUCE RICHARDSON, Introduction to *The Book of Tea*, 55

CHAPTER 2:
CULTIVATING ARTISTIC SKILLS IN OUR BASIC BEHAVIOR

This Chapter contains sections on each behavior: creating living space, obtaining food, eating, courting, having sex, parenting, grooming, playing, building, forming social bonds, fighting, fleeing, and sleeping.

Creating Living Space

These quotations pertain to land and landscaping. The section on Building has more quotations on living space.

Every plant has its fitness and must be placed in its proper surroundings so as to bring out its full beauty. Therein lies the art of landscaping.
JENS JENSEN, *Siftings*, 41

We humans have disrupted natural habitats in so many ways in so many places that the future of our nation's biodiversity is dim unless we start to share the places in which we live—our cities and, to an even greater extent, our suburbs—with the plants and animals that evolved there.
DOUGLAS TALLAMY, *Bringing Nature Home*, 286

[It] is not yet too late to save most of the plants and animals that sustain the ecosystems on which we ourselves depend. Second, restoring native plants to most human-dominated landscapes is relatively easy to do.
DOUGLAS TALLAMY, *Bringing Nature Home*, 9

If we are to balance and redirect our remarkable technological muscle power, we need to regain some ancient virtues: the humility to acknowledge how much we have yet to learn, the respect that will allow us to protect and restore nature, and the love that can lift our eyes to distant horizons, far beyond the next election, paycheque or stock

dividend. Above all we need to reclaim our faith in ourselves as creatures of the Earth, living in harmony with all other forms of life.
DAVID SUZUKI, *Sacred Balance*, 294

The natural world is the maternal source of our being as earthlings and life-giving nourishment of our physical, emotional, aesthetic, moral and religious existence. The natural world is the larger sacred community to which we belong. To be alienated from this community is to become destitute in all that makes us human. To damage this community is to diminish our own existence.
THOMAS BERRY, *The Dream of the Earth*, 81

Obtaining Food

Farming, animal husbandry, horticulture, and gardening, at their best, are complex and comely arts.
WENDELL BERRY, *Bringing It to the Table*, 233

1. Participate in food production to the extent that you can. If you have a yard or even a porch box or a pot in a sunny window, grow something to eat in it.... 2. Prepare your own food. This means reviving in your own mind and life the arts of kitchen and household.... 3. Learn the origins of the food you buy, and buy the food that is produced closest to your home.... The locally produced food supply is the most secure, the freshest, and the easiest for local consumers to know about and to influence. 4. Whenever possible, deal directly with a local farmer, gardener, or orchardist.... 5. Learn, in self-defense, as much as you can of the economy and technology of industrial food production. What is added to food that is not food, and what do you pay for these additions? 6. Learn what is involved in the *best* farming and gardening. 7. Learn as much as you can, by direct observation and experience if possible, of the life histories of food species.
WENDELL BERRY, *Bringing It to the Table*, 232

There is an inescapable kinship between farming and art, for farming depends as much on character, devotion, and the sense of structure, as on knowledge. It is a practical art. But it is also a practical religion, a

practice of religion, a rite. By farming we enact our fundamental connection with energy and matter, light and darkness. In the cycles of farming, which carry the elemental energy again and again through the seasons and the bodies of living things, we recognize the only infinitude within reach of the imagination.
WENDELL BERRY, *The Art of the Commonplace*, 285

Eating

To lead lives of artistry, we have only to slow down, to simplify, and return to the kitchen. For nothing is more intrinsically creative than cooking, which engages all the senses. Although we tend to consider the taste of food to be primary, our skills are needed in many different ways: we need to play with the colours of a dish... the textures of the food... and the different smells of cooking. Even sounds can be enticing.... The food itself, its presentation, the choice of serving dishes, the sequence of courses—all these elements carried out with mindfulness provide opportunities for creative choice.
JOHN LANE, *Timeless Simplicity*, 93

To speak of the pleasure of eating is to go beyond those categories [politics, esthetics, ethics]. Eating with the fullest pleasure—pleasure, that is, that does not depend on ignorance—is perhaps the profoundest enactment of our connection with the world.
WENDELL BERRY, *The Art of the Commonplace*, 326

As a community, we share not only a commitment to protect our natural resources, but an appreciation for the value of food itself, a love for its taste and beauty and the deep pleasure it can bring by connecting us to time and place, the seasons, and the cycle of nature.
ALICE WATERS, *The Art of Simple Food*, 4

They are the principles of a delicious revolution, one that can connect our families and communities with the most basic human values, provide the deepest delight for all our senses, and assure our well-being for a lifetime. Eat locally and sustainably.... Eat seasonally.... Shop at farmer's markets.... Plant a garden.... Conserve, compost, and recycle.... Cook

simply, engaging all your senses.... Cook together.... Eat together.... Remember food is precious.
ALICE WATERS, *The Art of Simple Food*, 5–7

Tending the soil, planting, and growing food in this way has had a long and important history in this country. If we let ourselves, we can easily return to this tradition. And what a revolutionary idea: That we can preserve the land by nurturing the vital link between taste, cooking, and gardening! It can be as simple as putting a seed in the ground and watching it grow.
ALICE WATERS, *The Art of Simple Food II*, 6

Treasure the farmer. Nurture the soil. Plant wherever you are. Learn from nature. Cultivate your palate. Make your own. Eat whole foods. Share the harvest. Teach children the art of simple food.
ALICE WATERS, *The Art of Simple Food II*, inside front cover

Courting

Happiness in marriage is not something that just happens. A good marriage must be created.... [That includes] giving each other an atmosphere in which each can grow. It is finding room for the things of the spirit. It is a common search for the good and the beautiful.
WILFERD PETERSON, *The Art of Living*, 86–87

Philosophers, poets, theologians, and most recently psychologists have tried to define the various forms of love. In the process, for all their good intentions, they've often scrambled each other's terms and definitions. My own way of understanding the different forms of love separates them into seven main kinds. The first is *aesthetic appreciation*. When we feel this emotion we are experiencing the object of our appreciation in an almost tactile way, drinking in its—or his or her—form, color, texture, sound, taste, and smell; but we're still somewhat emotionally distant. We feel wonder and satisfaction at the beauty we are experiencing, and the chemical fires are beginning to flicker; but they haven't been fanned into

the flames of passion yet. If that happens, they flare into the second form of love—*sexual attraction*.
DOUGLAS GILLETTE, *Primal Love*, 81

The human mind's most impressive abilities are like the peacock's tail: they are courtship tools, evolved to attract and entertain sexual partners. By shifting our attention from a survival-centered view of evolution to a courtship-centered view, I shall try to show how, for the first time, we can understand more of the richness of human art, morality, language, and creativity.... Our minds are entertaining, intelligent, creative, and articulate far beyond the demands of surviving on the plains of Pleistocene Africa.... By intelligently choosing their sexual partners for their mental abilities, our ancestors became the intelligent force behind the human mind's evolution.
GEOFFREY F. MILLER, *The Mating Mind*, 4

The study of aesthetic evolution requires engaging with both sides of sexual attraction: the object of desire and the form of desire itself, which biologists refer to as display traits and mating preferences.... What emerges from an understanding of the workings of sexual selection is the startling realization that desire and the objects of desire coevolve with each other.... It is through this coevolutionary mechanism that the extraordinary aesthetic diversity of the natural world comes into being. This book, then, is ultimately a natural history of beauty and desire.
RICHARD O. PRUM, *The Evolution of Beauty*, 8

Having Sex

The love I have always sought is ultimately full-bodied. For me, the erotic force that vibrates throughout all of nature has its finest human expression in the joining of bodies along with hearts, minds, and spirits. Through that joining, I have entered into states that can only be called religious. I have experienced alterations of perception, of time and space. I have sensed that absolute unity so celebrated in the literature of erotic love, a sense of oneness that extends not only to my lover but also to the larger world.
GEORGE LEONARD, *The End of Sex: Erotic Love after the Sexual Revolution*, 73

If both my love and I are fields of radiant energy, unique and irreducible, expressing the universe from particular points of view, then our joining is no casual matter. When the two of us come together in love, a new energy field is created, greater than and different from the sum of its parts.

GEORGE LEONARD, *End of Sex,* 152

High Monogamy is not for everyone, nor is it the only path to creative, transformative love. Sometimes the most fleeting erotic encounter can strike the chord of poignancy and delight that has the power to transform lives, and in youth a certain amount of erotic exploration is a natural urge. High Monogamy deserves a brief here simply because, in an age that is fascinated with erotic options, it is one option that is rarely mentioned. I define it as a long-term relationship in which both members are *voluntarily* committed to erotic exclusivity, not because of legal, moral or religious scruples, not because of timidity or inertia, *but because they seek challenge and an adventure*. High Monogamy requires, first of all, a goodly supply of self-esteem in both partners.... It is essential that both partners have mutual interests and share a common vision of life's purpose and how to achieve it.

GEORGE LEONARD, *End of Sex,* 153–54

Each usual man, with any like woman, can procreate others. Together, they have that magic capability. And when a pair select each other for that end, they can do so as procreative artists, with the most splendid and just hopes for their bodily creativity, or they can choose one another for some other and alien image in the mind,... We cannot even imagine what a splendor would burst upon us, males and females, if we reared both to be artists of the species by their loving.

PHILIP WYLIE, *The Magic Animal,* 268

Parenting

Every child is an artist. The problem is how to remain a child once we grow up.

PABLO PICASSO, source unknown

The object of education is to teach us to love what is beautiful.
PLATO, *The Republic*

In practicing the art of parenthood an ounce of example is worth a ton of preachment. Our children are watching us live, and what we *are* shouts louder than anything we can say.... Don't just stand there pointing your finger to the heights you want your children to scale. *Start climbing and they will follow!*
WILFERD PETERSON, *The Art of Living*, 96–97

It is essential that civilization should produce beautiful children.... we claim that schools should be institutions to help beauty, because beauty is an indication of health conditions of life.
MARIA MONTESSORI, *To Educate the Human Potential*, 114

Grooming

Visual beauty does not reign supreme in our sensual world—we are lured by beautiful voices, gestures of invitation, and sexy smells. We are even drawn to people by secretions from their hormones and immune systems that we cannot consciously detect. Looks are not everything, even in the superficial world of attraction and glances. But we are still left with the question of how to think about beauty.
NANCY ECTOFF, *Survival of the Prettiest: The Science of Beauty*, 241

All honour and reverence to the divine beauty of form! Let us cultivate it to the utmost in men, women, and children—in our gardens and in our houses. But let us love that other beauty too, which lies in no secret of proportion but in the secret of deep human sympathy.
GEORGE ELIOT, quoted by Nancy Ectoff, *Survival of the Prettiest*, 245

The character of a person expressed through a lively and mobile face is what really makes them attractive. The way we see people's faces is an active process. We are not passive recorders of the world around us. We select when we look—necessarily, because that is the way the brain works. In seeking, the eyes supply the brain with sensory data about the external world. But to make any sense of this data, the brain has to

interpret and organize it. We may be able to agree on judgements of a "physically beautiful face" but, beyond casual romance, our more committed choice of lover, partner or spouse is affected by our mind's filter of beliefs, prejudices, passions, fears, interests and blind spots. We see what our needs and desires allow us to see. In other words, in everyday life, we find attractive the people we like.
BRIAN BATES and JOHN CLEESE, The Human Face, 232

Playing

Play has a tendency to be beautiful. It may be that this aesthetic factor is identical with the impulse to create orderly form, which animates play in all its aspects. The words we use to denote the elements of play belong for the most part to aesthetics, terms with which we try to describe the effects of beauty: tension, poise, balance, contrast, variation, solution, resolution, etc. Play casts a spell over us; it is "enchanting," "captivating." It is invested with the noblest qualities we are capable of perceiving in things: rhythm and harmony.
JOHAN HUIZINGA, Homo Ludens: A Study of the Play-Element in Culture, 10

The great competitions in archaic cultures had always formed part of the sacred festivals and were indispensable as health and happiness-bringing activities. This ritual tie has now been completely severed; sport has become profane, "unholy," in every way and has no organic connection whatever with the structure of society, least of all when prescribed by the government. The ability of modern social techniques to stage mass demonstrations with the maximum of outward show in the field of athletics does not alter the fact that neither the Olympiads nor the organized sports of American Universities nor the loudly trumpeted international contests have, in the smallest degree, raised sport to a culture-creating activity. However important it may be for the players or spectators, it remains sterile. The old play-factor has undergone almost complete atrophy.
JOHAN HUIZINGA, Homo Ludens, 197–98

There is a deeper form of play, akin to rapture and ecstasy, that humans relish, even require to feel whole.
DIANE ACKERMAN, *Deep Play*, 12

Whole cultures play with customs, ideas, belief systems, and fashions. But it's a special caliber of play—*deep*—that leads to transcendence, creativity, and a need for the sacred.
DIANE ACKERMAN, *Deep Play*, 26

Neuroscientists, developmental biologists, social scientists, and researchers from every point of the scientific compass now know that play is a profound biological process. It has evolved over eons in many animal species to promote survival. It shapes the brain and makes animals smarter and more adaptable. In higher animals, it fosters empathy and makes possible complex social groups. For us, play lies at the core of creativity and innovation. Of all animal species, humans are the biggest players of all. We are built to play and built through play.
STUART BROWN, *Play*, 4-5

The ability to play is critical not only to being happy, but also to sustaining social relationships and being a creative, innovative person.
STUART BROWN, *Play*, 6

The human animal, being the most intelligent and opportunistic species in existence, is also the most playful. And, since this intelligence has given us a modern lifestyle in which survival is no longer a day-to-day problem, our playfulness has stretched more and more into the adult phase. The childlike adult has become the norm and amazing extensions of playfulness are all around us. Many of our social activities are mature forms of adult play. We go play-eating in our restaurants and play-drinking in our bars and pubs. As in all play, it is not the basic survival activities that are important but their playful exaggeration and ornamentation. Our playful curiosity has been elaborated into our arts and our scientific research. Play-hunting has become sport, acrobatic play has become dancing and gymnastics. Play-fighting has become politics. The names have been changed to make us feel more

sophisticated, but the playful roots of our greatest preoccupations are clear enough to any objective animal-watcher.
DESMOND MORRIS, *Animal Watching*, 235

This whole enterprise of improvisation in life and art, of recovering free play and creativity, is about allowing ourselves to be true to ourselves and our visions, and true to the undiscovered wholeness that lies beyond the self and the vision we have today. That is what quality is all about.
STEPHEN NACHMANOVITCH, *Free Play*, 177

In the original Olympics] prizes came to be offered for dance, poetic improvisation, speech-making, and music. There was even an Olympic prize for trumpet-sounding.
GEORGE LEONARD, *The Ultimate Athlete*, 172

My own view is that athletics is an art form. As a fan, I watch in the same way that I imagine an art connoisseur studies a painting.
BILL RUSSELL, quoted by George Leonard in *Ultimate Athlete*, 49

In creative lives, activities become deep play when they have at least one of four features. First, deep play is mentally absorbing.... Second, deep play offers players a new context in which to use some of the same skills they use in their work.... Third, deep play offers some of the same satisfactions as work, but it also offers different, clearer rewards thanks to differences in media or scale or pace.... Finally, deep play provides a living connection to the player's past.
ALEX SOOJUNG-KIM PANG, *Rest*, 201–2

The art of living is one and indivisible. It is not a composite art made up by adding the art of play to the art of work, or the art of leisure to the art of labour, or the art of the body to the art of the mind, or the art of recreation to the art of education. When life is divided into these or any other compartments it can never become an art, but at best a medley or at worst a mess. It becomes an art when work and play, labour and leisure, mind and body, education and recreation, are governed by a single vision of excellence and a continuous passion for achieving it.
LAWRENCE JACKS, *Education through Recreation*, 1–2

Building

The quest of organic architecture is to search for an objective beauty, a search for truth One of the things we teach young architects at Taliesin is the importance of sensitivity to details in daily life, such as placing fresh flowers on the dining tables. We urge them to be constantly conscious of the beauty of their surroundings, to seek opportunities to create something beautiful.
JOHN RATTENBURY, *A Living Architecture*, 67

I believe a house is more a home by being a work of Art.
FRANK LLOYD WRIGHT, *The Natural House*, 226

To develop the art and science of a more natural design, we can look to nature itself and discover what shapes it.
LANCE HOSEY, *The Shape of Green*, 33

Every designer everywhere can: 1. Bridge the divide between "good design" and "green design." 2. Turn beauty and sustainability into the same thing. 3. Erase the distinction between how things look and how things work. 4. Break down the walls between the arts and sciences. 5. Adopt the three principles: *Conserve*: Shape things to respect resources. *Attract*: Shape things to be easy to use and deeply satisfying. *Connect*: Shape things to embrace place. 6. Start with the napkin sketch, not the technical manual. 7. Develop a scientific method for design. 8. Strengthen the ties between form and performance, between image and endurance. 9. Make things to work as well and to last as long as they should. 10. Make things better.
LANCE HOSEY, *Shape of Green*, 179–80

An elegant solution is in a class all its own, that what sets it apart is the unique combination of surprising power and uncommon simplicity, and that elegance entails achieving far more with much less when faced with a complex problem. Elegance is indeed a widely sought-after quality, and yet it takes many forms.
MATTHEW E. MAY, *In Pursuit of Elegance*, 16

More and more, people are beginning to return to the almost forgotten Renaissance era of mastery. They're adopting a different view of their work. In all walks of professional life, from senior executives to factory workers to part-timers people are beginning to see themselves as artists and scientists.
MATTHEW E. MAY, *The Elegant Solution*, 15

Forming Social Bonds

We can create fulfilling relationships by engaging in the preceding behaviors with artistic skill. We learn to form those bonds from our families, friends, mentors, teachers, writers, others, and our choices.

Fighting and Fleeing

We can channel our aggression energy into learning artistic skills and creating beautiful lives. In *The End of War*, John Horgan argued persuasively that we can end war. In *Why Civil Resistance Works*, Erica Chenoweth and Maria Stephan observed that between 1900 and 2006, nonviolence was more effective than violence.

Sleeping

Everyone knows how to do it [rest], but with a little work and understanding, you can learn to do it a lot better.... Many notable creatives do their most intense work early in the morning when their minds are freshest and least prone to distraction. They go on walks or take naps during the day to revive and maintain their energy while allowing their subconscious minds time to wander and explore.
ALEX SOOJUNG-KIM PANG, *Rest*, 14–15

It is a common experience that a problem difficult at night is resolved in the morning after the *committee of sleep* has worked on it.
JOHN STEINBECK, quoted by Dierdre Barrett in *The Committee of Sleep*, ix

CHAPTER 3:
LINKING ART, SCIENCE, AND RELIGION

Artistic, *scientific*, and *religious* can refer to artistic skill, scientific knowledge, and religious experience. Highly developed skills are called *artistic*. Adequately reliable knowledge is called *scientific*. Sufficiently deep experiences are called *religious*. Science and religion can help us learn artistic skills in the art of living.

In theory, to create beautiful lives, we need to learn everyday and specialized forms of art, science, and religion. The everyday forms modify our basic behavior as we go about our daily lives. They are skills in the art of living, scientific knowledge learned while practicing those skills, and religious devotion to learning those skills.

The specialized forms are the fine arts, the social and natural sciences, and organized religion. Our appreciation of and participation in these specialized forms can help us learn the everyday forms.

All religions, arts and sciences are branches of the same tree. All these aspirations are directed toward ennobling man's life, lifting it from the sphere of mere physical existence and leading the individual toward freedom.
ALBERT EINSTEIN, Out of My Later Years, 9

In my view, it is the most important function of art and science to awaken this [religious] feeling and keep it alive in those who are receptive to it.
ALBERT EINSTEIN, Ideas and Opinions, 38

Science, like art and religion, is a product of cognitive fluidity.... Early Humans could not use metaphor because they lacked cognitive fluidity. But for Modern Humans, analogy and metaphor pervade every aspect of our thought and lie at the heart of art, religion and science.... the potential arose in the mind to undertake science, create art and believe in religious ideologies.
STEVEN MITHEN, The Prehistory of the Mind, 246

[*Quality* is] a rational basis for a unification of the three areas of human experience which are now disunified. These three areas are Religion, Art, and Science.
>ROBERT PIRSIG, *Zen and the Art of Motorcycle Maintenance*, 257

We have artists with no scientific knowledge and scientists with no artistic knowledge and both with no spiritual sense of gravity at all, and the result is not just bad, it is ghastly.
>ROBERT PIRSIG, *Zen and the Art of Motorcycle Maintenance*, 294

By tracing in broad outline the evolution of art, science, religion, philosophy, and social thought during the last 500 years, I hope to show that during this span the peoples of the West offered the world a set of ideas and institutions not found earlier or elsewhere. As already remarked, it has been a unity combined with enormous diversity. Borrowing widely from other lands, thriving on dissent and originality, the West has been the mongrel civilization par excellence. But in spite of patchwork and conflict, it has pursued characteristic purposes—that is its unity—and now these purposes, carried out to their utmost possibility, are bringing about its demise. This ending is shown by the deadlocks of our time: for and against nationalism, for and against individualism, for and against the high arts, for and against strict morals and religious beliefs.
>JACQUES BARZUN, *From Dawn to Decadence*, xix

The radiant images of religion and of art as well as of science... emerge from the depths of consciousness.
>HAVELOCK ELLIS, *The Dance of Life*, 102

The longer I am in the "professional pursuit of religion," if you want to call it that, the more I discover the great importance of art and of science for the fullness of human life.
>FRITJOF CAPRA and DAVID STEINDL-RAST, *Belonging to the Universe*, 6

The sense in which "moral" means something to me is the sense in which religion, science, and art operate out of the same nucleus. The moral

value is then compassionate, true, and enacted; a mystery of physical and psychic coordination is embodied in it.
        M. C. RICHARDS, *Centering in Pottery, Poetry, and the Person*, 142

The complex relations among art, science, and religion are vital for me.
        THOMAS MATUS, quoted in *Belonging to the Universe*, 6

There is a perfect identity of physics, mathematics, religion, and great art.
        OSWALD SPENGLER, quoted by Havelock Ellis in *The Dance of Life*, 131

Creativity is our birthright. It is an integral part of being human, as basic as walking, talking, and thinking. Throughout our evolution as a species, it has sparked innovations in science, beauty in the arts, and revelation in religion. Every human life contains its seeds and is constantly manifesting it, whether we're building a sand castle, preparing Sunday dinner, painting a canvas, walking through the woods, or programming a computer. The creative process, like a spiritual journey, is intuitive, non-linear, and experiential. It points us toward our essential nature, which is a reflection of the boundless creativity of the universe.
        JOHN LOORI, *The Zen of Creativity*, 1.

In religion and art, mystery is light itself. It's the lifeblood that pumps through true religious and artistic practice. Mystery is the itch that you can't scratch, the driving force of spiritual and creative journeys. It sets in motion the basic questions of our existence. It fuels genuine scientific investigation.
        JOHN LOORI, *The Zen of Creativity*, 192

The metaphor of the cosmic dance thus unifies ancient mythology, religious art, and modern physics.
        FRITJOF CAPRA, *The Tao of Physics*, 233

The sequence of a period of distress followed by illumination is a characteristic human pattern which,... can be discerned in the process of

creative discovery in the arts and the sciences, and also in religious conversion.
          ANTHONY STORR, *Feet of Clay*, 175

It will be seen that the revival of religion on a scientific basis does not mean the death of art, but a glorious rebirth of it.
       GEORGE BERNARD SHAW, Preface, *Back to Methuselah*, xci

This oceanic feeling of wonder is the common source of religious mysticism, of pure science and art for art's sake; it is their common denominator and emotional bond.
        ARTHUR KOESTLER, *The Act of Creation*, 258

What integrates an individual life is a consistent creative purpose or unconscious direction. Instinct alone will not suffice to give unity to the life of a civilized man or woman: there must be some dominant, an ambition, a desire for scientific or artistic creation, a religious principle, or strong and lasting affections.
     BERTRAND RUSSELL, *Principles of Social Reconstruction*, 158

[Psychosynthesis] has the virtues of being open to the great contributions of science, art and the spiritual traditions.
          PIERO FERRUCCI, *What We May Be*, 15

The three main pillars of culture, art, science, and spirituality had become too compartmentalized and this was one of the fundamental causes of the fragmentation of contemporary thought today. If these three domains were able to recognize their interfaces clearly, it could provide a solid basis for the wholeness craved for by so many people.
   LOUWRIEN WIJERSs, *Art Meets Science and Spirituality*, edited by Andreas Papadakis, Louwrien Wijers and Johan Pijnappel, 83

The task facing art is enormous: art, genuine art, guided by religion, with the help of science, must make it so that men's peaceful life together, which is now maintained by external measures—courts, police, charitable institutions, workplace inspections, and so on—should be

achieved by the free and joyful activity of men. Art should eliminate violence. And only art can do that.
LEO TOLSTOY, *What is Art?* 165–66

Science and art are like those barges with kedge-anchors, "machines" as they were called, that used to work our rivers. Like the boats that carry the anchor ahead and drop it, science prepares for the movement, the direction of which is given by religion, while art is like the winch worked from the barge, which, by pulling the barge to the anchor, accomplishes the movement itself.... The degree of importance both of the feelings conveyed by art and of the knowledge conveyed by science is determined for people by the religious consciousness of the given time and society—that is, the general understanding among people of that time and society of the purpose of their life.
LEO TOLSTOY, *What is Art?* 157–58

If the day ever dawns when science, art, and religion become as one by recognizing each other's faculties as different in reality, but really as reinforcing each other, we would then have something like the thing which is now missing.
FRANK LLOYD WRIGHT, in *Frank Lloyd Wright*, by Olgivanna Wright, 94

Civilization has got to be something more than it has been if it's ever going to be the great blessing and great joy that it might be, where art and religion join hands with science and all three get together, it would really make life beautiful.
FRANK LLOYD WRIGHT, "The Seasons of Civilization," a talk to Taliesin apprentices recorded in 1954

Science and art and even religion must find expression, as one, in what we build.
FRANK LLOYD WRIGHT, *An Organic Architecture*, 10

Organic architecture is no mere aesthetic nor cult nor fashion but an actual movement based on a profound idea of a new integrity of human life wherein art, religion and science are one.
FRANK LLOYD WRIGHT, *An Organic Architecture*, 47

Wright looked for the day when those involved in art, science and religion realized that their interest and source of inspiration are one and the same.
JOHN RATTENBURY, *A Living Architecture*, 16–17

All the wisdom of science, the cunning of politics, and the prayers of religion can but stand and wait for the revelation—awaiting at the hands of the artist "conventionalization," that free expression of life-principle which shall make our social living beautiful.
FRANK LLOYD WRIGHT, *Frank Lloyd Wright Collected Writings*, vol. 1, Bruce Brooks Pfeiffer, editor, 125

No man is free who is afraid, and he's afraid until he has developed the certainty that comes of a creative life, and a creative role in life, by way of art, religion, and science. The real body of the universe is spiritual.... Man is chiefly animal and until he makes something of himself by way of the spirit and becomes spiritual and aware, he's not creative, he can't be, until science and art and religion are more or less one, we're not going to be safe.
FRANK LLOYD WRIGHT, interview on June 18, 1957; https://openculture.com

Science, philosophy, religion, and art are forms of knowledge. The method of science is experiment; the method of philosophy is speculation; the method of religion and art is moral or aesthetic *emotional* inspiration. But both science and philosophy, religion and art, begin to serve *true* knowledge only when in them commence to manifest the sensing and finding of some inner property of things.... [The] divisions into science, philosophy, religion, and art betray the poverty and incompleteness of each. A complete religion unites in itself religion, art, philosophy, and science; a complete art equally unites them, while a complete science or a complete philosophy comprehends religion and art. A religion which contradicts science, and a science which contradicts religion are both equally false.
P. D. OUSPENSKY, *Tertium Organum: A Key to the Enigmas of the World*, 208

Discussion of politics and religion may be banned at the dinner-table and at the officer's mess, but it would surely be a mockery to attempt any

study of the arts and sciences, especially in their historical aspects, without reference to such controversial issues. My aim has been to find the highest common factors in art, science, and religion. To these basic concepts any particular art or science or religion will, of course, be able to add its own particular glory.
>> PHILIP A. COGGIN, *Art, Science, and Religion*, 10

It will be evident that Mr. Coggin has the philosophic mind and knows how to cultivate it in the class-room,... so that a youngster may truly think like a scientist, see and feel like an artist and know the inwardness of religion.
>> BASIL YEAXLEE, "Towards Wholeness," *British Journal of Religious Education*, vol. 2, no. 4 (1963): 30

The religious outlook is the sum of all our outlooks. To say that a man has no religion has meaning only in the sense that he has never tried to add all his experiences together into a sum-total—in short, to probe the meaning and purpose of life.
>> PHILIP A. COGGIN, *Art, Science, and Religion*, 181

If we can develop scientific, aesthetic, and religious methods of dealing with the experiences and phenomena that confront us, the facts will look after themselves.
>> PHILIP A. COGGIN, *Art, Science, and Religion*, 9

It is the appreciation of the ultimate mystery, whether in science or art or life, that is the kernel of religion.
>> PHILIP A. COGGIN, *Art, Science, and Religion*, 81

Art, like science, is a religious activity, because it is concerned with an aspect of reality. Neither is enough by itself, because each gives only a partial view. Both are needed as well as their applications, and when they come together so that the individual self responds to the whole of its environment, religion appears in all its fullness.... Science and art need religion to give meaning and purpose, and to preserve the balance between the various parts of man's work, life, and personality. Equally, religion needs science and art, for both are concerned with the fearless

pursuit of truth, and a religion which cannot benefit from the relentless scrutiny of science or the illuminating sincerity of art is likely to be a godless superstition.
       PHILIP A. COGGIN, *Art, Science, and Religion*, 83–84

By a proper education I mean an education that has taught him [the student] to adapt himself to the world in which he will live. His aim must be, not to master a subject or subjects, but to master the method of dealing with this world. By stressing the points of contact between art, science, and religion, I have tried to show that fundamentally there exists only one method, and this, in a universe whose basic unity is becoming more and more obvious through the discoveries of science, is as it should be.
       PHILIP A. COGGIN, *Art, Science, and Religion*, 179

I tried to show earlier that science and art are religious activities because they are concerned with creation in its material manifestation as well as in the spiritual significance underlying it. If this is true, then an education which is not religious has no meaning. By a religious education I mean one that pursues truth as an ideal greater than, and independent of, the individual. Such truth must therefore be approached with humility and reverence. In most religions such truth is equated with God, and the contemplation of it will result in awe and wonder and worship.
       PHILIP A. COGGIN, *Art, Science, and Religion*, 177

  The following quotations link art and science with mysticism, and mystical experiences are often religious:

The most beautiful and most profound emotion we can experience is the sensation of the mystical. It is the sower of all true science.
  ALBERT EINSTEIN, in *The Universe and Dr. Einstein* by Lincoln Barnett, 105

Science, art, and mysticism also share the modest claim that their "truths" are tentative and incomplete, never absolute and inerrant The effort to plumb the mysteries of existence, the simple effort to know, is what has created all the arts, science, and religions.... The studies of

science, of the arts, and of mysticism are studies of the same subject: the world. At this deepest level, science, art, and the inward way are united.
STEVEN FORTNEY and MARSHALL ONELLION, *Seeking Truth: Living with Doubt*, 24

So what would a society look like that is leavened by these beliefs that unite science, art, and mysticism? It would look exactly like the world scientific investigation has disclosed to us, with the addition of the warmth and humanity of art, the adventure of the creative mind, the speculative breadth of the religious impulse. All in all, not a bad place to live.
STEVEN FORTNEY and MARSHALL ONELLION, *Seeking Truth: Living with Doubt*, 183

Particularly in China and India, there has been a difficult but attractive ideal of the man who is, at once, a mystic, an artist, and a scientist in the sense of knowing all there is to know. As a variety of the Indian ideal, that of the aristocratic Javanese unites the aesthetic and the mystical, both of which are superlatively civilized to him, or, in his terminology, *alus*.
BEN-AMI SCHARFSTEIN, *Mysticism*, 95

Creation, then, whether internal or external, mystical, scientific, or artistic, expresses the need for unity.
BEN-AMI SCHARFSTEIN, *Mysticism*, 97

The rediscovery of ancient mysticism in Florence led to an extraordinary flowering of arts and science known as the Renaissance, meaning "rebirth," which laid the foundation for our modern age.
TIMOTHY FREKE and PETER GANDY, *Complete Guide to World Mysticism*, 74

By the term "cosmology" I mean three things: a scientific story about the origins of our universe; mysticism that is a psychic response to our being in a universe; and art, which translates science and mysticism into images that awaken body, soul, and society. A cosmology needs all three elements to come alive: it is our joyful response (mysticism) to the

awesome fact of our being in the universe (science) and our expression of that response by the art of our lives and citizenship (art).
MATTHEW FOX, *The Coming of the Cosmic Christ*, footnote on page 1

Consider a new paradigm to be a new wineskin. One does not harvest a new crop of grapes, crush them, and pour them into old, dried-up wineskins. Rather, one seeks a new wineskin that is supple and soft, giving and forgiving, flexible and eager to be made wet, one that welcomes newness and creativity. Such a wineskin is the living cosmology being blended from three rich vineyards: science, from which we derive a universal creation story today; mysticism, from which we awaken the human psyche's powers for unity, wholeness, and imagination; and art, from which the Good News of a living cosmology is born into the hearts, dreams, imaginations, and bodies of persons, and even into the institutions of the culture.
MATTHEW FOX, *The Coming of the Cosmic Christ*, 162

When science, mysticism, and art come together again, our worship will delight, amaze, allure, and empower us.
MATTHEW FOX, *Creation Spirituality*, 37

The following quotations describe how art, science, and religion were united in the distant past. For example, a healing ritual may have combined an artistic skill (e.g., chanting, singing, or dancing) with scientific knowledge (e.g., herbal remedy) and religious experience (e.g., profound devotion).

Originally, science, art, and religion were not distinct but were inseparably united. Considering that these three have such a deep significance throughout human history, it seems clear the present gulf between them must have a harmful effect in the generative order of the consciousness of humanity. But there is no intrinsic reason why those three attitudes have to be separated. Rather, while one of them may be emphasized in a particular activity, the others must always be present although, for the moment, they may be in the background. Nevertheless humanity has become conditioned to accept such a rigid separation. What is clearly needed is a dialogue between these attitudes, in which

sooner or later they can all come into the "middle ground" between them, which will make available a new order of operation of the mind with rich possibilities for creation. The opening of such a dialogue could play a crucial role in freeing the consciousness of humanity from one of the most significant blocks to creativity.
    DAVID BOHM and F. DAVID PEAT, *Science, Order, and Creativity*, 265

[Our concept of art] is the outcome of the social process of two thousand years, the result of the breakup of the classic tradition of thought into various parts which under post-classic influences have been pursued separately. Religion or the desire for the salvation of our souls, "Art" or the desire for beautification, Science or the search for the reasons of things—these conations of the mind, which are really three aspects of the same profound impulse, have been allowed to furrow each its own narrow channel, in alienation from the others, and so they have all been impeded in their greater function of fertilizing human life.
    HAVELOCK ELLIS, *The Dance of Life*, 7–8

People of our time possess four ways that lead to the Unknown, four forms of conception of the world—religion, philosophy, science and art. These ways diverged long ago. And the very fact of their divergence shows their remoteness from the source of their origin, that is from esotericism. In ancient Egypt, in Greece, in India, there were periods when the four ways constituted one whole.
    P. D. OUSPENSKY, *A New Model of the Universe*, 33

Greek art and Greek science fitted in happily with Greek religion; indeed, religion did much to inspire and sustain the poets and philosophers.
    C. W. BOWRA, *Classical Greece*, 17

CHAPTER 4:
SEEKING BEAUTY, TRUTH, AND GOODNESS

Art, science, and religion can be paths toward the ancient ideals of beauty, truth, and goodness. Art can be a path toward beauty, science a path toward truth, and religion a path toward goodness. Each path can eventually lead toward all three ideals.

What do those three words mean? Let us begin with simple, essential dictionary meanings. *Beauty* can mean harmony. *Truth* can mean knowledge of reality. *Goodness* can mean morality. Let us add to those meanings only those that help us seek the ancient ideals. Note that we can seek the ancient ideals without defining them, and we can cooperate seeking them without agreeing on definitions.

Art for art's sake is an empty phrase. Art for the sake of the true, art for the sake of the good and the beautiful, that is the faith I am searching for.
GEORGE SAND (Amantine Dupin), quoted in *The Wisdom of Women*, edited by Carol Spenard La Russo, 78

Beauty, truth, and goodness pursued for their own sakes would give us a working definition of art, science, and morality. These three ideals have represented man's highest aspirations in every age and in every country. All three have defied attempts to explain their origin, to define them in unambiguous terms, and even to justify their existence. Truth, however, is not the prerogative of science, nor beauty of art. If the world is a unity, then nothing can be separated in a literal sense. When we say that beauty is truth and truth beauty we are not saying that beauty and truth are identical. They are complementary aspects of the same thing, and you cannot point to where one begins and the other leaves off. They interact inextricably. So with art and science. They are not indistinguishable, but in their highest reaches it may well be difficult to tell which is which.
PHILIP A. COGGIN, *Art, Science, and Religion*, 68

The ideal of the artist is beauty... the ideal of the scientist is truth, and of the moralist, goodness. Any one of these ideals is worth the devotion of a lifetime,... yet no one of them alone can satisfy man's thirst for wholeness. In Hindu thought, these three comprise the qualities of the soul. If they are indeed within us, then the work of the artist, the scientist, and the moralist or social reformer is a response to an inner urge and an inner vision that must be in some degree present before he takes up his career. The total vision, which comprises all three—beauty, truth, and goodness—is what we call religion. The wholeness from which such a vision proceeds, we call God.... True worship lies in recognizing the holiness of wholeness.

BRADFORD SMITH, *Meditation: The Inward Art*, 80

It is likely that the word "religion" is based upon the same root that gives us ligament and ligature, So it means to tie, to bind. Dictionaries usually derive the word from re-, meaning back, and lig-, meaning to bind. But re- also means anew. "To bind anew." Isn't this what religion really tries to do?—to bind truth and beauty and goodness together in one vision, to make us aware of wholeness, and thus to make us whole?

BRADFORD SMITH, *Meditation*, 80

For who can doubt, really, that a view of the universe not restricted by our human limitations would disclose that reality as it is intimated to us through truth, beauty and goodness—through art, science, and religion—would turn out to be a unity far more perfect than we can imagine, and far more beautiful?

BRADFORD SMITH, *Meditation*, 93

The scientist probes the universe looking for truth, the artist for beauty, the moralist for goodness. All have faith in the truth, the beauty or the goodness they look for. Without this faith they could not work. Inherent in the universe is a summation of all its meaning. If we could see it plain, we would perhaps then realize that truth, beauty, and goodness are also only aspects of the total meaning. Yet our human limitations leave us always with a partial view. We are left with the paradox of unity in diversity, of error in good, of blemish in beauty, or truth that may be eternal but for us is progressive because it is being continuously revealed. And we have to learn to be content with a situation in which our human limitations leave us with all these paradoxes, and with the

knowledge that in all these paradoxes and beyond them is the unity we call God.
BRADFORD SMITH, *Meditation*, 203–4

Plato's vision [was] that the good, the true, and the beautiful are the fabric of reality.
RENEE WEBER, *Dialogues with Scientists and Sages: The Search for Unity*, 13

The affirmation of goodness, truth and beauty as fundamental attributes of the universe is a legacy left to us by the sages of Greece and the seers of India. In its most coherent form, the doctrine has been traditionally identified with Plato, whose idealistic cosmology, metaphysics and ethics have carried it down to use from the 4th century BC. Far from being obsolete, Plato's triadic characterization of the cosmos is arousing renewed interest because unexpectedly contemporary science has arrived at some parallel conclusions.
RENEE WEBER, "The Good, the True, the Beautiful", *The Theosophical Journal* (December 1985)

When Plato considered the great trilogy of Beauty, Truth, and Goodness, he placed Beauty at the top because Beauty is harmony, and whether Truth or Goodness is harmonious is the test of their integrity. Goodness gives a person self-respect, Truth gives gratification, but Beauty gives both peace and joy simultaneously. Plato believed that Goodness, or ethics, consists of acting in a way that is harmonious with your fellow human beings, and this makes the action testable by its beauty.
ROLLO MAY, *My Quest for Beauty*, 27

The union of beauty with goodness and truth has been common enough to be regarded as natural. It is the dissociation which is unnatural and painful.
JOHN CROWE RANSOM, *The World's Body*, 72

The ideals which have lighted my way, and time after time have given me new courage to face life cheerfully, have been Kindness, Beauty, and Truth.
ALBERT EINSTEIN, *Ideas and Opinions*, 9

In their labors they [the religious] will have to avail themselves of those forces which are capable of cultivating the Good, the True, and the Beautiful in humanity.
>   ALBERT EINSTEIN, *Ideas and Opinions*, 48

My awareness of belonging to the invisible community of those who strive for truth, beauty, and justice has prevented me from feelings of isolation.
>   ALBERT EINSTEIN, quoted in *Einstein*, by John Gribbin and Michael White, 262

The goal of humanistic studies was defined as the perception and knowledge of the good, the beautiful, and the true. Such studies were expected to refine the discrimination between what is excellent and what is not (excellence generally being understood to the true, the good, and the beautiful). They were supposed to inspire the student to the better life, to the higher life, to goodness and virtue.
>   ABRAHAM MASLOW, *Religions, Values, and Peak-Experiences*, 8

Since the dawn of history, every known civilization has developed a conception of which statements are true and which are false; which experiences are considered to be beautiful, ugly, or banal; and which human actions and relationships are deemed good, compromised, or frankly evil. Human beings reached a crucial milestone when they began explicitly to speak and write about these virtues and their lack: In the founding texts of the Hebrew Bible, the Confucian Analects, the Vedic Upanishads we find telling references to important truths, examples of beautiful language and images, and clear identification of good and evil. And a high point arrived when the philosophers of Athens—preeminently Socrates, Plato, and Aristotle—laid out explicitly their own definitions of truth, beauty, and goodness and what it means to lead lives guided by this set of virtues.
>   HOWARD GARDNER, *Truth, Beauty, and Goodness Reframed*, 5

The trio of virtues, while unquestionably in flux and under attack, remain essential to the human experience and, indeed, to human survival. They must not and will not be abandoned.
>   HOWRD GARDNER, *Truth, Beauty, and Goodness Reframed*, 13

The ancient Greeks relied preeminently on reason to seek, with Plato, the True, the Good, and the Beautiful.
STUART KAUFFMAN, *Reinventing the Sacred*, xii

All people live—consciously or unconsciously—on the strength of their principles, their ideals; that is, by virtue of what they regard as truth, beauty, and goodness. Many get their ideal all ready-made, in definite, historically-developed forms. They live trying to square their lives with this ideal, deviating from it at times, under the influence of passions or incidents, but neither reasoning about it or questioning it. Others, on the contrary, subject it to the analysis of their own reason.
IVAN TURGENEV, in *Essays of the Masters*, edited by Charles Neider, 380

Our exploration of Truth, Goodness, and Beauty has thus far focused on divine, cosmic, and human frames of reference that began with the pre-Socratics, were developed in the philosophy of Plato, and were radically reappropriated in the formative period of the Christian tradition. Common to all these traditions is the idea that Truth, Goodness, and Beauty are cosmic values that awaken within us our true humanity.
STEPHEN TURLEY, *Awakening Wonder*, 50

Truth, goodness, and beauty form a triad of terms which have been discussed together throughout the tradition of western thought. They have been called "the three fundamental values" with the implication that the worth of anything can be exhaustively judged by reference to these three standards.
MORTIMER J. ADLER, *A Syntopicon: An Index to the Great Ideas,* 88

Distinctively, the Indo-European thinkers worked with the conviction, or at least the hypothesis, that being is convertible with truth, goodness, oneness, and beauty. These are European Christian scholastic terms (known as the "transcendentals," the qualities that apply to beings always and everywhere, in virtue of being itself), but they have their equivalents in Hinduism and Buddhism, as well as in Greek-influenced Judaism and Islam.
DENISE CARMODY and JOHN CARMODY, *Mysticism*, 298–99

The process of perception, as discussed earlier (pp. 80–110), involves thinking about (or "knowing"), affective responding to, and enactive interaction with the world. The three aspects of the natural world that particularly resonate with these three aspects of perception are truth, beauty, and goodness respectively. They also resolve with the subject matter of core philosophical areas of enquiry: metaphysics, aesthetics, and ethics. This suggests that the triad of truth, beauty, and goodness—which already has a long history of use in this context—might constitute a helpful scheme around which to organize a theological engagement with nature.

ALISTER MCGRATH, The Open Secret, 221–22

The Christian tradition is familiar; it is "home" for me. I was born into it and grew up in it. Its stories, language, music, and ethos are familiar. It nurtured me, even as I have had to unlearn some of what I was taught.... For me, it mediates the good, the true, and the beautiful; and through all of these it mediates the sacred. It is for me a sacrament of the sacred.

MARCUS BORG, The Heart of Christianity, 223

And this power revealed itself not merely as the Beauty, which underlies all the forms of nature; not merely as the Truth which philosophy discerns beneath the appearances of things; but as a moral power, a power of Good.

BEDE GRIFFITHS, The Golden String, 78

Moral animals [humans] are inescapably interested in and guided by normative cultural orders that specify what is good, right, true, beautiful, worthy, noble, and just in life, and what is not.

CHRISTIAN SMITH, Moral, Believing Animals, 153

Each and every human being who has ever brought anything of beauty, value, or importance into the world has done so only because that individual has been impregnated or in-spirited by some aspect of Beauty, Truth, Love, or other attributes of God.

MICHAEL DOWD, Thank God for Evolution, 363

From the Arts I have learnt about truth and beauty, enchantment and imagination, thanksgiving and transcendence, balance and shamanic power. They have brought new worlds into being. They are the very food of my humanity. In fact I find it difficult to conceive of what it would be like to live in the absence of this treasury of revelations.
JOHN LANE, *Timeless Simplicity*, 84

The great classic triumvirate of Truth, Beauty and Goodness is a particularly apt framework for engaging C. S. Lewis and philosophy. These magnificent ideals are not only at the heart of the classic philosophical enterprise, the tradition into which Lewis was initiated in his Oxford philosophical training, but they are also of crucial significance in the Christian vision of reality he came to embrace.
JERRY WALLS, in *C. S. Lewis as Philosopher*, edited by David Baggett, Gary Habermas, and Jerry Walls, 17

It is our hope that they [C. S. Lewis essays] will not only honor his philosophical contributions but also enable us in our day to show the power and glory of Truth, Beauty, and Goodness and the splendor of the One in whom they are perfectly joined.
JERRY WALLS, in *C. S. Lewis as Philosopher*, edited by David Baggett, Gary Habermas, and Jerry Walls, 19

For the ancient wisdom schools as well as for the earliest universities, the quest for cosmic order, expressed as justice, lay at the center of their learning. Thus the "is-ness" and the "ought-ness" of life were understood as integral to one another. Virtue was inherent in and inseparable from truth, beauty, and goodness.
JIM GARRISON, in *New Thought, Ancient Wisdom* by Glenn Mosely, 69–70

What if we said that the Beautiful, the Good, and the True are dimensions of your very own being at each and every moment, including each and every level of growth and development? And that through an integral practice, you can discover deeper and deeper dimensions of your own Goodness, your own Truth, and your own Beauty?
KEN WILBER, *Integral Spirituality*, 19

Truth, Goodness, and Beauty are thus, in varying degrees, the fundamental concerns of art and therefore ought to be the fundamental concerns of criticism. Otherwise criticism must be irrelevant.
>> JOHN GARDNER, *On Moral Fiction*, 144

True art is *by its nature* moral. We recognize true art by its careful, thoroughly honest search for and analysis of values. It is not didactic because, instead of teaching by authority and force, it explores, open-mindedly, to learn what it should teach. It clarifies, like an experiment in a chemistry lab, and confirms. As a chemist's experiment tests the laws of nature and dramatically reveals the truth or falsity of scientific hypotheses, moral art tests values and rouses trustworthy feelings about the better and the worse in human action.
>> JOHN GARDNER, *On Moral Fiction*, 19

Beauty is integrity, goodness, and truth.
>> JIDDU KRISHNAMURTI, in *The Beauty of the Mountain*, by Friedrich Grohe, xvi

Logic follows Ethics and both follow Aesthetics.
>> CHARLES SANDERS PEIRCE, *Collected Papers of Charles Sanders Peirce*

In the infancy of society every author is necessarily a poet, because language itself is poetry; and to be a poet is to apprehend the truth and the beautiful, in a word, the good which exists in the relation subsisting, first between existence and perception, and secondly between perception and expression.
>> PERCY BYSSHE SHELLEY, *A Defense of Poetry and Other Essays*, 49

If the sense of beauty, then, is the gentle guide both to truth and to goodness, and if beauty itself, as defined in this book, is that inner principle, what are the implications for our present moment in history? Evidently it is incumbent on us, it is our good duty, to nurture the creative process of nature and to continue it in our own good work.... The new age that is coming will fall into that class of historical periods that we call renaissances—periods when past wisdom and beauty are recovered, inspiring radical innovation and changes.
>> FREDERICK TURNER, *Beauty: The Value of Values*, 135

Beauty is the *radiance* of the true and good, and it is what attracts us to both.
STRATFORD CALDECOTT, *Beauty for Truth's Sake*, 31

Our humanity is bound up with our capacity to realize that Being (and therefore everything that exists, in one degree or another) is one, good, true, and beautiful. When we are brutalized into ignorance of this fact, or denied the experience of it, the taste of it, then we have become less than human.
STRATFORD CALDECOTT, *Beauty in the* Word, 135

The infant is brought to consciousness of himself only by love, by the smile of his mother. In that encounter, the horizon of all unlimited being opens itself for him, revealing four things to him: (1) that he is one in love with the mother, even in being other than his mother, therefore all being is one; (2) that that love is good, therefore all Being is good; (3) that that love is true, therefore all Being is true; and (4) that that love evokes joy, therefore all Being is beautiful.
HANS URS VON BALTHASAR, *My Work in Retrospect*, 114

Not too many years from now, it seems safe to predict, people who love literature, music, and painting for their power to express beauty, truth, and the good will once again dominate the faculties of the world's leading universities and set the tone for public conversation about artistic excellence.
CHARLES MURRAY, *Human Accomplishment*, 456

You can make a creative contribution to this time in history by giving your support to the good and the true and the beautiful. You can take a new look at your work and make creative changes. You can look at human needs and help supply creative answers.
WILFERD PETERSON, *The Art of Creative Thinking*, 91

When we reflect on the realms of the true, the good, and the beautiful, we find that they are in some sense mutually inclusive. Each realm, in a way, embraces and unifies the scope of human reason. All three are unified within the realm of the true.... But all three are also unified within

the realm of the good.... Finally, all three are unified within the realm of the beautiful.
MONTAGUE BROWN, *Restoration of Reason*, 239

Without a minimum of common assurances, it is not possible for men to live together in society. If they are not to massacre each other, men must agree on a certain number of fundamental questions: what is good, what is evil; what is true, what false; what is beautiful, what ugly.
IGNAZIO SILONE, "Ferrero and the Decline of Civilizations," in *Essays of the Masters*, edited by Charles Neider, 330

All creatures bear a certain resemblance to God, most especially man, created in the image and likeness of God. The manifold perfections of creatures—their truth, their goodness, their beauty—all reflect the infinite perfection of God.
Catechism of the Catholic Church, Section 41. See *Wisdom* 13:5.

In Christian theology the transcendentals are treated in relation to Theology Proper, the doctrine of God. The transcendentals, according to Christian doctrine, can be described as the ultimate desires of man. Man ultimately strives for perfection, which takes form through the desire for perfect attainment of the transcendentals. The Catholic Church teaches that God is Himself Truth, Goodness, and Beauty.
"Transcendentals" (2015, June 26). In *Wikipedia: The Free Encyclopedia. Retrieved September 5, 2015, from* https://en.Wikipedia.org/w/index.php?title=Transcendentals&oldid=668770073

Truth, and goodness, and beauty, are but different faces of the same All.
RALPH WALDO EMERSON, *Essential Writings of Ralph Waldo Emerson*, 13

For the Universe has three children, born at one time, which reappear under different names in every system of thought, whether they be cause, operation, and effect;... These stand respectively for the love of truth, for the love of good, and for the love of beauty. These three are equal. Each is that which he is, essentially, so that he cannot be surmounted or analyzed, and each of these three has the powers of the others in him and his own, patent.
RALPH WALDO EMERSON, *Essential Writings of Ralph Waldo Emerson*, 289

In the eternal trinity of Truth, Goodness, and Beauty, each in its perfection including the three, they prefer to make Beauty the sign and head.
RALPH WALDO EMERSON, *Essential Writings of Ralph Waldo Emerson*, 93

You must, from your own observation, from your own sense of what is right and beautiful, good and true, make your own statement.
FRANK LLOYD WRIGHT, quoted in *A Living Architecture*, John Rattenbury, 27

We instinctively feel the good, true, and beautiful to be essentially one in the last analysis. Within us there is a divine principle of growth to some end; accordingly we select as good whatever is in harmony with this law.
FRANK LLOYD WRIGHT, *Frank Lloyd Wright Collected Writings*, vol. 1, edited by Bruce Brooks Pfeiffer, 104

The expression we seek and need is that of harmony or of the good, known otherwise as the true, often spoken of as the beautiful, and personified as God.
FRANK LLOYD WRIGHT, *The Essential Frank Lloyd Wright*, edited by Bruce Brooks Pfeiffer, 72

Because religious humanists believe that whatever is good, true, and beautiful is part of God's design, they have confidence that their faith can assimilate the works of culture. Assimilation, rather than rejection or accommodation, constitutes the heart of the religious humanist's vision.
GREGORY WOLFE, *The New Religious Humanists*, xvi

Public discourse has increasingly come to be dominated by warring academic elites; there are fewer and fewer men and women of "letters"— non-academic artists and writers who balance a passion for truth and goodness with the concreteness that beauty demands.
GREGORY WOLFE, *Beauty Will Save the World*, xiii

In art, beauty takes the hard edges off truth and goodness and forces them down to earth, where they have to make sense or be revealed as

imposters.... I've become an advocate for beauty as the necessary agent for rendering the claims of truth and goodness meaningful.
GREGORY WOLFE, Beauty Will Save the World, xiv

The essence of all art is to have pleasure in giving pleasure.
MIKHAIL BARYSHNIKOV

Truth, Goodness, Beauty—those celestial thrins,
Continually are born; e'en now the Universe,
With thousand throats, and eke with greener smiles,
Its joy confesses at their recent birth.
HENRY DAVID THOREAU, Journals, June 14, 1838

The following quotations link beauty and goodness. If these statements are true, then they link beauty and goodness with truth:

The great moral teachers of humanity were, in a way, artistic geniuses in the art of living.
ALBERT EINSTEIN, Ideas and Opinions, 51

Painting is not done to decorate apartments.... It is an instrument of war against brutality and darkness.
PABLO PICASSO

Beauty will save the world!
FYODOR DOSTOEVSKY, The Idiot, 351

The perception of beauty is a moral test.
HENRY DAVID THOREAU, journal entry, September 1850; quoted in *Thoreau and the Art of Life*, by Roderick MacIver, 29

Examine each question in terms of what is ethically and aesthetically right, as well as what is economically expedient. A thing is right when it tends to preserve the integrity, stability, and beauty of the biotic community. It is wrong when it tends otherwise.
ALDO LEOPOLD, Sand County Almanac, 224–25

Aesthetics and ethics are both words that come from the Greek language, and the Greeks did not distinguish the sphere of aesthetics from the sphere of ethics.
JOHN RATTENBURY, *A Living Architecture*, 65

But if there is a food politics, there are also a food esthetics and a food ethics, neither of which is dissociated from politics.
WENDELL BERRY, *Bringing It to the Table*, 229

New technologies come to our aid in understanding the relation of beauty to goodness. Brain imaging can show where the aesthetic experience is located: Indeed, when we perceive beauty, the cerebral region that is activated is the same one as when we make moral choices and judgments or is contiguous to it. In other words, beauty and goodness are roommates in our brain.
PIERO FERRUCCI, *Beauty and the Soul*, 170

The Navaho language uses the word *hozho*, which means health, beauty, goodness, harmony, and happiness, all at once. Here the dualism between the beautiful and the good, prevalent in our culture, disappears. Beautiful and good are the same thing. And so also success and happiness. The prefix "ho" means whole and infinite, and thus gives the idea of harmony with the environment and the universe. Navaho thought does not make any distinction between humans and nature. In this culture people are encouraged continually to walk amid beauty, speak in beauty, act in beauty, and live in beauty.
PIERO FERRUCCI, *Beauty and the Soul*, 173

The great secret of morals is love; or a going out of our own nature, and an identification of ourselves with the beautiful which exists in thought, action, or person, not our own. A man, to be greatly good, must imagine intensely and comprehensively; he must put himself in the place of another and of many others; the pains and pleasures of his species must become his own.
PERCY BYSSHE SHELLEY, *In Defense of Poetry and Other Essays*, 54

Art, all art, has in itself the property of uniting people. All art causes those who perceive the feeling conveyed by the artist to unite in soul, first with the artist, and secondly with all who have received the same impression.

LEO TOLSTOY, *What Is Art?* 129

Art is that human activity which consists in one man's consciously conveying to others, by certain external signs, the feelings he has experienced, and in others being infected by those feelings and also experiencing them.... [Art] is a means of human communion, necessary for life and for the movement towards the good of the individual man and of mankind, uniting them in the same feelings.

LEO TOLSTOY, *What Is Art?* 40

Art should eliminate violence. And only art can do that. All that presently makes it possible for men to live together, independently of the fear of violence and punishment... has been brought about by art.... Art should make it so that the feelings of brotherhood and love of one's neighbour,... become habitual feelings, an instinct for everyone.... And uniting the most diverse people in one feeling and abolishing separation, the art of the whole people will educate mankind for union, will show them, not by reasoning but in life itself, the joy of general union beyond barriers set up by life.... People's well-being lies in being united among themselves and in establishing, in place of the violence that now reigns, that Kingdom of God—that is, of love which we all regard as the highest aim of human life.

LEO TOLSTOY, *What Is Art?* 166–67

Look first at the connection between beauty as "fairness" and justice as "fairness," using the widely accepted definition by John Rawls of fairness as a "symmetry of everyone's relations to each other." The discussion will then turn to the idea of "aliveness," a word that, though it enters our discussions of justice less openly and less often than words such as "fairness" and "equality," is what is centrally at stake in, and served by, both spheres.

ELAINE SCARRY, *On Beauty and Being Just*, 93

Plato believed that Goodness, or ethics, consists of acting in a way that is harmonious with your fellow human beings, and this makes the action testable by its beauty. Indeed, the Greek word for beauty and for goodness is the same, "*kalon*."... And when Socrates gave his enchanting prayer at the conclusion of *Phaedrus*, "O Pan, and all ye other Gods that haunt this place, give me beauty in the inward mean, and may the outward and inward man be at one," he was illustrating again that ethics follows beauty.
ROLLO MAY, *My Quest for Beauty*, 27–28

Nothing is more hallowing than the union of kindred spirits in art.... At the moment of meeting, the art lover transcends himself. At once he is and is not. He catches a glimpse of Infinity, but words cannot voice his delight, for the eye has no tongue. Freed from the fetters of matter, his spirit moves in the rhythm of things. It is thus that art becomes akin to religion and ennobles mankind.
KAKUZO OKAKURO, *The Book of Tea*, 100

Many scientists now believe that moral perceptions are akin to aesthetic or sensual perceptions, emanating from many of the same regions of the brain.... You don't have to decide if a landscape is beautiful. You just know. Moral judgments are in some ways like that. They are rapid intuitive evaluations.
DAVID BROOKS, *The Social Animal*, 285

It is one of the most beautiful compensations of life that no man can sincerely try to help another without helping himself.
RALPH WALDO EMERSON

Go deep enough into your experience to find that beauty is in itself the finest kind of morality—ethical, purely—the essential fact, I mean, of all morals and manners.
FRANK LLOYD WRIGHT, in *Frank Lloyd Wright Collected Writings*, vol. 1, edited by Bruce Brooks Pfeiffer, 117

Instinctively and naturally, if you beautify your own life, you beautify the life of everyone around you.
FRANK LLOYD WRIGHT, in *Frank Lloyd Wright on Architecture, Nature, and the Human Spirit*, edited by Bruce Brooks Pfeiffer, 61

To recognize the identity of beauty and holiness is to get rid of a confusion which has plagued aestheticians for centuries.
JOHN GARDNER, *On Moral Fiction*, 156

Art's incomparable ability to instruct, to make alternatives intellectually and emotionally clear, to spotlight falsehoods, insincerity, foolishness—art's incomparable ability, that is, to make us understand—ought to be a force bringing people together, breaking down barriers of prejudice and ignorance, and holding up ideals worth pursuing.
JOHN GARDNER, *On Moral Fiction*, 42

Great art celebrates life's potential, offering a vision unmistakably and unsentimentally rooted in love. "Love" is of course another of those embarrassing words, perhaps a word even more embarrassing than "morality," but it's a word no aesthetician ought carelessly to drop from his vocabulary... the single quality without which true art cannot exist.
JOHN GARDNER, *On Moral Fiction*, 83

Frost was right in claiming that the choice of each image in a poem is a moral choice, but only because it is the poet's obligation to make no bad choice if he can help it. The immorality of an inept poet is like that of a sleeping guard or a drunken bus driver.
JOHN GARDNER, *On Moral Fiction*, 144

The creative genius of Van Gogh was simply loving what he saw and then wanting to share it with others, not for the purpose of showing off, but out of generosity.
BRENDA UELAND, *If You Want to Write*, 21

If you read the letters of the painter Van Gogh, you will see what his creative impulse was. It was just this: He loved something—the sky, say.

He loved human beings. He wanted to show human beings how beautiful the sky was. So he painted it for them. And that was all there was to it.
BRENDA UELAND, *If You Want to Write*, 18

The best way to know the Truth or Beauty is to try to express it. And what is the purpose of existence Here or Yonder but to discover truth and beauty and express it, i.e., share it with others?
BRENDA UELAND, *If You Want to Write*, 179

Art is a mode of prediction not found in charts and statistics, and it insinuates possibilities of human relations not to be found in rule and precept, admonition and administration.
JOHN DEWEY, *Art as Experience*, 349

Imagination is the chief instrument of the good. It is more or less a commonplace to say that a person's ideas and treatment of his fellows are dependent upon his power to put himself imaginatively in their place. But the primacy of the imagination extends far beyond the scope of direct personal relationships. Except where "ideal" is used in conventional deference or as a name for a sentimental reverie, the ideal factors in every moral outlook and human loyalty are imaginative. The historic alliance of religion and art has its roots in this common quality. Hence it is that art is more moral than moralities.
JOHN DEWEY, *Art as Experience*, 348

Were art an acknowledged power in human association and not treated as the pleasuring of an idle moment or as a means of ostentatious display, and were morals understood to be identical with every aspect of value that is shared in experience, the "problem" of the relation of art and morals would not exist.
JOHN DEWEY, *Art as Experience*, 348

Humanistic ethics, for which "good" is synonymous with good for man and "bad" is bad for man, proposes that in order to know what is good for man we have to know his nature. *Humanistic ethics* is the applied science of the "art of living" based upon the theoretical "science of man."
ERICH FROMM, *Man for Himself*, 18

CHAPTER 5:
MYSTICAL EXPERIENCE

Mystical experiences of deep peace and profound unity can occur during artistic and scientific creativity and during religious experience.

In theistic traditions [mysticism is] often described as a fundamental unitive experience of love and communion with God, in non-theistic traditions as a unitive, contemplative approach to ultimate reality.... Examples of mystical experience can be found throughout the world's religions.... Common to them is the insistence on an experience of fundamental unity or oneness transcending the diversity of everyday life.
Penguin Dictionary of Religions, 333

This overcoming of all the usual barriers between the individual and the Absolute is the great mystic achievement. In mystic states we both become one with the Absolute and we become aware of our oneness. This is the everlasting and triumphant mystical tradition, hardly altered by differences of clime or creed. In Hinduism, in Neoplatonism, in Sufism, in Christian mysticism, in Whitmanism, we find the same recurring note, so that there is about mystical utterances an eternal unanimity which ought to make a critic stop and think, and which brings it about that the mystical classics have, as has been said, neither birthday nor native land. Perpetually telling of the unity of man with God, their speech antedates languages, and they do not grow old.
WILLIAM JAMES, *The Varieties of Religious Experience*, 457

The great religious mystics who, like the great scientists and artists, interpret the universe for those who are less gifted, do not hesitate to attribute this feeling of oneness between the self and the universe to the existence of what they call God in a man's inner self, and to the existence of God in the universe.
PHILIP A. COGGIN, *Art, Science, and Religion*, 79

During these [mystical] moments the self, the ego (one's separateness) disappears, melts, as the individual fuses experientially with the object(s)

of perception: the cosmos or nature, his work—especially when he is producing an object or working on a craft—sometimes even with another,... The great religious figures and saints were *mystics* as I use the term. The great artists and poets are, as well, and they communicate their experiences to others through their work.... My interest was and is purely in that elevated moral sense, intuitional mind, and unitive consciousness described in the great scriptural, literary and poetic works of humankind.
MARSHA SINETAR, *Ordinary People as Monks and Mystics*, 5–6

Mystics almost universally report an "illumination" as part of their experience, but it is usually an illumination within the context of the world view to which they are committed (or which they have absorbed through their culture).
ANDREW GREELEY, *Ecstasy: A Way of Knowing*, 18.

Mystical experience is the direct, unmediated experience of what Bede Griffiths beautifully describes as "the presence of an almost unfathomable mystery... which seems to be drawing me to itself." This mystery is beyond name and beyond form; no name or form, no dogma, philosophy, or set of rituals can ever express it fully.
ANDREW HARVEY, *The Essential Mystics*, x

What do we suggest as a working description of mysticism? We suggest: "direct experience of ultimate reality." "Ultimate reality" can connote "God," "the Tao," "*nirvana*," "the sacred," or any of the other terms that religious people have coined to indicate what is unconditioned, independent of anything else, most existent, dependable, valuable.
DENISE CARMODY and JOHN CARMODY, *Mysticism*, 10

This is not a time for denominational one-upmanship. It is a time to cull wisdom from any and all of its sources and to let folly go. Even and including religious folly. One reason I depend in this book so heavily upon mystical writings is offered by Carl Jung, when he observed that "it is only the mystic who brings creativity to religion." If we are to make our faiths live again—not for their own sakes but for the survival of our species—then we had better become mystically literate again.
MATTHEW FOX, *One River, Many Wells*, 8

Spirituality, like religion, derives from mysticism. For thousands of years before the dawn of the world religions as social organisms working their way through history, the mystical life thrived. This mystical tradition, which underpins all genuine faith, is the living source of religion itself. It is the attempt to possess the inner reality of the spiritual life, with its mystical, or direct, access to the divine. Each great religion has a similar origin: the spiritual awakening of its founders to God, the divine, the absolute, the spirit, Tao, boundless awareness.... Everything stems from mysticism, or primary religious experience, whether it be revelation or a personal mystical state of consciousness.... Religions are valuable carriers of the tradition within a community.
WAYNE TEASDALE, The Mystic Heart, 10–11

Mysticism means direct, immediate experience of ultimate reality. For Christians, it is union and communion with God. For Buddhists, it is realization of enlightenment.
WAYNE TEASDALE, The Mystic Heart, 20

Mysticism is where religions start. Moses with his flocks in Midian, Buddha under the Bo tree, Jesus up to his knees in the waters of Jordan, each of them is responding to Something of which words like *Shalom*, *Nirvana*, *God* even, are only pallid souvenirs. Religion as ethics, institution, dogma, ritual, Scripture, social action, all of this comes later and in the long run maybe counts for less. Religions start, as Frost said poems do, with a lump in the throat—to put it mildly—or with a bush going up in flames, a rain of flowers, a dove coming down out of the sky. "I have seen such things," Thomas Aquinas told a friend, "that make all my writings seem like straw." Most people have also seen such things. Through some moment of beauty or pain, some sudden turning of their lives, most of them have caught glimmers at least of what the saints are blinded by. Only then, unlike the saints, they tend to go on as though nothing has happened. We are all more mystics than we choose to let on, even to ourselves.
FREDERICK BUECHNER, Wishful Thinking, 77

Mysticism is the deepest level of spirituality.
TIMOTHY FREKE, Spiritual Traditions, 153

Mysticism. A name for the perennial spiritual philosophy. Mysticism teaches that the supreme reality cannot be known by thoughts, but only through direct experience. Mystics emphasize the underlying unity of all things, and recognize other religions as different ways of approaching the same truth.
TIMOTHY FREKE, *Spiritual Traditions*, 249

The natural experience of spiritual awakening that lies at the heart of mysticism is the birthplace of all religions, and they find their common ground in this common source.
TIMOTHY FREKE and PETER GANDY, *Complete Guide to World Mysticism*, 15

Mysticism begins with the extraordinary experiences of the ancient shamans of the primal peoples who, through the use of ritual and psychedelic plants, began an exploration of the mysteries of consciousness. In India this wisdom flowered into a profound philosophy which gradually influenced the whole of the ancient world. Ancient Egypt also developed a similar mysticism, which gave birth to the Mystery Schools—spiritual "universities" for mystical initiation. The philosophies of India and Egypt came together in ancient Greece. Here, the Mystery Schools flourished as a religion for a thousand years, and left a legacy that would inspire all subsequent Western mystics.
TIMOTHY FREKE and PETER GANDY, *Complete Guide to World Mysticism*, 16

Some mystics describe the experience as one of union in which self and God merge indistinguishably, others as a communion in which self and God interpenetrate but "particularity" somehow remains, a difference generally (though not universally) characteristic of Eastern and Western mysticism respectively.
MARCUS BORG, *Days of Awe and Wonder*, 66

The heart of creativity is an experience of the mystical union; the heart of mystical union is an experience of creativity.
JULIA CAMERON, *The Artist's Way*, 2

The seventeenth-century German philosopher Gottfried Leibnitz coined the phrase *philosophia perennis*, and it was popularized in the twentieth century by the British author Aldous Huxley (who wrote a book titled *The Perennial Philosophy*) and others. The perennial philosophy holds that the world's great spiritual traditions, in spite of their obvious differences, express the same fundamental truth about the nature of reality, a truth that can be directly apprehended during a mystical experience.

JOHN HORGAN, *Rational Mysticism*, 17

Each of the Abrahamic faiths [Judaism, Christianity, Islam] had its mystics who discerned creation as the material manifestation of an undifferentiated spiritual unity rather than the handiwork of an aging patriarch who lives apart from his creation. The cosmologies of Western mystics bear more than a passing resemblance to those of the mystics of Eastern religious traditions, particularly of Buddhism and Hinduism, who make little distinction between humans and nature.

DAVID KORTEN, *Change the Story, Change the Future*, 48–50

I see in the history of many organized religions a tendency to develop two extreme wings: the "mystical" and individual on the one hand, and the legalistic and organizational on the other. The profoundly and authentically religious person integrates these trends easily and automatically.

ABRAHAM MASLOW, *Religions, Values, and Peak-Experiences*, vii

The great lesson from the true mystics, from the Zen monks, and now also from the Humanistic and Transpersonal psychologists—that the sacred is *in* the ordinary, that it is to be found in one's daily life, in one's neighbors, friends, and family, in one's back yard.

ABRAHAM MASLOW, *Religions, Values, and Peak-Experiences*, x

Of all the contemporary psychologists who have addressed themselves to mystical phenomena, Abraham Maslow is the most sympathetic and the most perceptive, and his book *Religions, Values, and Peak-Experiences* (Ohio State University, 1964) ought to be read by those interested in the mystical phenomena.

ANDREW M. GREELEY, *Ecstasy: A Way of Knowing*, 19

The arts, while creating order and meaning from the seeming chaos of daily existence, also nourish our craving for the mystical.
> E. O. WILSON, *Consilience: The Unity of Knowledge*, 232

The [mystic] mind reflects in certain ways in order to reach ever higher levels of enlightenment until finally, when no further progress is possible, it enters a mystical union with the whole.
> E. O. WILSON, *Consilience: The Unity of Knowledge*, 260

Men of science endowed with the religious temperament are to-day reinterpreting the mystical meaning of the universe; and it is they who may bring about a new synthesis between our discovery of the true and our self-dedication to the beautiful and the good.
> BEATRICE WEBB, essay in *Living Philosophies,* 305

PART II:
SOCIAL SCIENCE

CHAPTER 6:
THE NEED FOR A NEW SOCIAL SCIENCE

Knowledge from social science has vastly expanded our understanding of human life. Nevertheless, eminent scientists criticize the current rate of progress. We might agree that social science could better help us seek to attain our highest potential and solve our social and ecological crises.

What does a history of the human sciences show? Succinctly, it is *diversity*.... Writers sometimes follow the language of the historian of science Thomas S. Kuhn, and describe psychology and the other human sciences as in a pre-paradigmatic stage. By this they mean that they accept that, *as yet*, there is no single unified theory, model of research practice and social identity for a field.
ROGER SMITH, The Norton History of the Human Sciences, 21–22

It is obvious to even casual inspection that the efforts of social scientists are snarled by disunity and a failure of vision. And the reasons for the confusion are becoming increasingly clear. Social scientists by and large spurn the idea of the hierarchical ordering of knowledge that unites and drives the natural sciences. Split into independent cadres, they stress precision in words within their specialty but seldom speak the same technical language from one specialty to the next. A great many even enjoy the resulting overall atmosphere of chaos, mistaking it for creative ferment. Some favor partisan social activism, directing theory into the service of their personal political philosophies.
E. O. WILSON, Consilience: The Unity of Knowledge, 182

The development of a vocabulary and syntax (or method) to enable scholars, policy makers, and citizens to talk fruitfully about societies and their relations is still a pressing priority in social science.
—Daniel Rossides, *Comparative Societies: Social Types and Their Interrelations*, 4

Although they [social sciences] were founded in the 18th and 19th centuries amid every expectation they would soon produce intellectual

discoveries, grand "laws," and validated theories to rival those of the rest of science, such success has remained elusive. The recent wave of antiscientific sentiment spreading through the social sciences draws much of its appeal from this endemic failure. This disconnection from the rest of science has left a hole in the fabric of our organized knowledge of the world where the human sciences should be. After more than a century, the social sciences are still adrift, with an enormous mass of half-digested observations, a not inconsiderable body of empirical generalizations, and a contradictory stew of ungrounded, middle-level theories expressed in a babel of incommensurate technical lexicons. This is accompanied by a growing malaise, so that the single largest trend is toward rejecting the scientific enterprise as it applies to humans.
JOHN TOOBY and LEDA COSMIDES, *The Adapted Mind*, 23

In the subset of the human sciences called social sciences the picture today seems gloomy. Economics has become more and more powerful as an ideological defense of and justification for the expanding free market without counterbalancing restraints. Sociology departments have tilted increasingly to the pursuit of ephemeral data collecting and statistical analyses so beloved of funding agencies that want "hard" results. Anthropologists are enamored of cultural studies with major political implications. Historians place the highest value on monographic research, based on archives.
BRUCE MAZLISH, *The Uncertain Sciences*, xv

The future of the human sciences appears unpromising. On one side, we are faced with a positivism that functions in faint imitation of its relatively successful use in the natural sciences. On the other side, we are confronted by phenomena that call for a hermeneutic method. The status of that method, however, is problematic. In sum, the use of an effective scientific method along the lines of positivism is handicapped, and the employment of the interpretive method highly unreliable.
BRUCE MAZLISH, *The Uncertain Sciences*, 129

CHAPTER 7:
BEAUTY IN SOCIAL SCIENCE

Many social scientists focus on our potential for experiencing and creating beauty. Expanding that emphasis might lead to an increased rate of progress in research.

Social Science in General

Given an infinite number of theories that will logically explain the facts, scientists will sensibly always choose the most beautiful theory. For good reason: this is the way the world works. Beauty in this view is the highest integrative level of understanding and the most comprehensive capacity for effective action. It enables us to go with, rather than against, the deepest tendency or theme of the universe.
FREDERICK TURNER, The Culture of Hope, 218

Scientists and humanists alike should remember to elaborate not only the truth of their discoveries but the beauty of what has been discovered. Of all the elements of learning, the perception of beauty is at once the most delightful and the most suggestive of an underlying principle that unites the disciplines. Beauty is the lingua franca of all learning and therefore must be at the core of successful pedagogy.
ROBERT GRUDIN, The Grace of Great Things, 163

Recurrent references to "beauty" across the sciences suggest a new interest in this abstract idea as a link between the disciplines. As a unifying abstraction, the sense of beauty may conceivably spread to the social sciences and beyond, unfolding new topics of discourse and an aesthetic dimension in fields previously considered value free.
ROBERT GRUDIN, The Grace of Great Things, 195

There are millions of people around the world already tapping into the arts and aesthetics for health and wellness. In order for the field of neuroarts to reach its full potential and become accessible to everyone, it will need to be sustained and supported. This means that there must be an increase in interdisciplinary research, in training and education for diverse practitioners, in new public and private policies, and in funding. There also needs to be accurate and ongoing communication, both within the field and with the general public, on how to talk about this work and to bring the arts and aesthetics into our lives. The good news is that we're already seeing strong global initiatives emerging around the arts and aesthetics. All disciplines from public health and education to business and technology are integrating the arts into their fields.

    SUSAN MAGSAMEN and IVY ROSS, *Your Brain on Art*, 240-41

Specific Social Sciences

Psychology

Self-actualizing people are, without one single exception, involved in a cause outside their own skin, in something outside of themselves. They are devoted, working at something, something which is very precious to them—some calling or vocation in the old sense, the priestly sense, they are working at something which fate has called them to somehow and which they work at and which they love, so that the work-joy dichotomy in them disappears. One devotes his life to the law, another to justice, another to beauty or truth..... the truth, and beauty and goodness of the ancients.

    ABRAHAM MASLOW, *Religions, Values, and Peak-Experiences*, 42.

These most mature of all people [self-actualizing] were also strongly childlike. These same people, the strongest egos ever described and the most definitely individual, were also precisely the ones who could be most easily ego-less, self-transcending, and problem-centered. But this is precisely what the great artist does. He is able to bring together clashing colors, forms that fight each other, dissonances of all kinds, into a unity. And this is also what the great theorist does when he puts puzzling and inconsistent facts together so that we can see that they really belong together. And so also for the great statesman, the great therapist, the great philosopher, the great parent, the great inventor. They are all integrators, able to bring separates and even opposites together into

unity. We speak here of the ability to integrate and of the play back and forth between integration within the person, and his ability to integrate whatever it is he is doing in the world. To the extent that creativeness is constructive, synthesizing, unifying, and integrative, to that extent does it depend in part on the inner integration of the person.
        ABRAHAM MASLOW, *Motivation and Personality* (third edition), 162

I couldn't decide whether my subjects [self-actualizing people] were selfish or unselfish. Observe how spontaneously we fall into an either-or here. The more of one, the less of the other is the implication of the style in which I put the question. But I was forced by sheer pressure of fact to give up this Aristotelian style of logic. My subjects were very unselfish in one sense and very selfish in another sense. And the two fused together, not like incompatibles, but rather in a sensible, dynamic unity or synthesis very much like what Fromm has described in his classical paper on healthy selfishness. My subjects had put opposites together in such a way as to make me realize that regarding selfishness and unselfishness as contradictory and mutually exclusive is itself characteristic of a lower level of personality development. So also in my subjects were many other dichotomies resolved into unities.
        ABRAHAM MASLOW, *Motivation and Personality* (third edition), 161–62

As he [Maslow] wrote in his 1962 book *Toward a Psychology of Being*: "Self-actualization.... paradoxically makes more possible the transcendence of self, and of self-consciousness and selfishness."
        SCOTT BARRY KAUFMAN, *Transcend*, xv.

The perception of beauty is a definition of perfect psychological health. The moment we perceive beauty in its fullness and we are filled with it, in that moment, even if only for that moment, we are not paranoid anymore, we are not depressed, we are not obsessive, we are not bitter. We are as we were meant to be.
        PIERO FERRUCCI, *Beauty and the Soul*, 128

Beauty is a primary principle that touches all parts and functions of our being. It opens us to the world and brings harmony to our relation with others and with nature; it helps us reach out and touch the entire universe.
PIERO FERRUCCI, *Beauty and the Soul*, xxvii

Everybody, to some extent, and more or less consciously, has since childhood been a seeker of beauty.
PIERO FERRUCCI, *Beauty and the Soul*, 175

The more we can perceive beauty in our surroundings, and also inside us, the more we will feel at home and glad to exist.
PIERO FERRUCCI, *Beauty and the Soul*, 31

To discover what is beautiful for us, and to enjoy it, is a potent aid, usually accessible if we stop resisting and just try—or if someone reminds us. We all find our own way, often in nature, or art, but also through some kind of self-expression, through relationships with others, in everyday life.
PIERO FERRUCCI, *Beauty and the Soul*, 9.

In order for our aesthetic intelligence not to atrophy, a much stronger engagement is needed, so that beauty, instead of occasional pastime, or a pleasant but transient novelty, becomes the basis of our life, a value shared by all.
PIERO FERRUCCI, *Beauty and the Soul*, 171.

He [Roberto Assagioli] was the first to emphasize the importance of beauty in the field of psychology.
PIERO FERRUCCI, *Beauty and the Soul*, xvi.

Sociology

The capacity to recognize beauty, the esthetic sense, is the primary cognitive skill of the historian or sociologist.
FREDERICK TURNER, *Rebirth of Value*, 149

If such a new idea system [new approach in sociology] does appear, to give new life and impetus to the realities of contemporary Western society, it will not be the consequence of methodology, much less of computers, of mass data gathering and retrieval, or of problem definition however rigorous, or research design however aseptic. It will be the consequence, rather, of intellectual processes which the scientist shares with the artist: iconic imagination, aggressive intuition, each given discipline by reason and root by reality. So it has always been and so it is now in those contemporary intellectual areas of most intense creativity. Foremost is the passion for reality—reality not obstructed by layers of conventionalization, but reality that is direct and unmediated.
       ROBERT A. NISBET, *The Sociological Tradition*, 318–19

What the distinguished mathematician Marston Morse has written is an appropriate note on which to conclude a book about Tocqueville, Marx, Weber, and Durkheim: "The creative scientist lives in 'the wilderness of logic' where reason is the handmaiden and not the master.... The more I study the interrelations of the arts the more I am convinced that every man is in part an artist. Certainly as an artist, he shapes his own life, and moves and touches other lives. I believe that it is only as an artist that man knows reality. Reality is what he loves, and if his love is lost, it is his sorrow.
       ROBERT A. NISBET, *The Sociological Tradition*, 319

The creation of Utopias—and their exhaustive criticism—is the proper and distinctive method of sociology.... Sociologists cannot help making Utopias.
  H. G. WELLS, "The So-Called Science of Sociology," *Sociological Papers* 3: 367

This synergy principle is so important, not only for a general objectively comparative sociology,... not only because it furnishes a scientific basis for utopian theory, but also for more technical social phenomena in other areas.
  ABRAHAM MASLOW, "Synergy in the Society and in the Individual," *Journal of Individual Psychology* 20, no. 2: 161

Societies where nonaggression is conspicuous have social orders in which the individual by the same act and at the same time serves his own advantage and that of the group. The problem is one of social engineering and depends upon how large the areas of mutual advantage are in any society. Nonaggression occurs not because people are unselfish and put social obligations above personal desires but because social arrangements make these two identical.... I shall need a term for this gamut, a gamut that runs from one pole, where any act or skill that advantages the individual at the same time advantages the group, to the other pole, where every act that advantages the individual is at the expense of others. I shall call this gamut *synergy*, the old term used in medicine and theology to mean combined action. In medicine, it meant the combined action of nerve centers, mental activities, remedies, which by combining produced a result greater than the run [sum?] of their separate actions. I shall speak of cultures with low synergy, where social structure provides for acts that are mutually opposed and counteractive, and of cultures with high synergy, where it provides for acts that are mutually reinforcing.

    RUTH BENEDICT, "Synergy: Some Notes of Ruth Benedict," *American Anthropologist*, article by Abraham Maslow and John J. Honigman, 325–26

We need to push forward to a less cautious and more imaginative engagement with possible futures, in which utopia is understood as a creative form of sociology.

RUTH LEVITAS, *Utopia as Method*, 149

Utopia does not require the imaginative construction of whole other worlds. It occurs as an embedded element in a wide range of human practice and culture—in the individual and collective creative practices of art as well as in its reproduction and consumption.

RUTH LEVITAS, *Utopia as Method*, 5

Note on Social Psychology

The following quotation suggests (1) that psychologists are social psychologists who study our individual lives, and (2) that sociologists are social psychologists who study our social lives:

The history of social psychology has most often been conceived in terms of the emergence of a specialist area within the overall discipline of psychology. This definition prejudges the way to think about the individual's relation to society. If, as some theorists argue, it is not possible even to formulate a concept of the individual independently of social categories and, conversely, if it is not possible to describe social existence without presuppositions about the physical and moral autonomy of human beings, then social psychology might be thought, in principle, to be the general discipline and the foundation of specialist subdisciplines like psychology and sociology.
     ROGER SMITH, *The Norton History of the Human Sciences*, 747–48

Economics

Let us accept responsibility for our self-aware agency and learn the arts of living in a conscious interconnected world. And let us rethink and restructure our institutions to find our place of contribution to creation's continual unfolding.
     DAVID C. KORTEN, *Change the Story, Change the Future*, 141–42

Human beings develop to their fullest potential in structured activities. And that is what business is fundamentally all about: the art of creating, maintaining, and refining structures of relationships and activities in which human beings can grow, prosper, and live life to the fullest. This is the beauty of business.
     TOM MORRIS, *If Aristotle Ran General Motors*, 100

We all have to contribute in our own ways toward providing the proper soil and nutrients for human beings to grow as people, and to develop as artists themselves at work. And this is true at every level of corporate life.... the aesthetic is everybody's business. Everyone in each of our business environments should be a partner for living well. The beauty and artistry of the workplace is everybody's business. And in this way, reinventing corporate spirit and reestablishing a new foundation for sustainable excellence in modern business is everybody's job.
     TOM MORRIS, *If Aristotle Ran General Motors*, 100

The economic value of goods depends on how much they are desired, and desirability depends on other values, such as aesthetic, moral, or veridical ones; these are generated by the creativity of human beings and of the rest of nature.
                              FREDERICK TURNER, *The Culture of Hope*, 119

The profit motive is like appetite: a normal, valuable, and indispensable drive for a living organism. When critics of capitalism use the terms "profit" and "profit motive," they do not distinguish between the healthy and the diseased forms of profit. The former is the result of the creation of new value, by ideas, art, science, and technology through which the pie is enlarged, while the latter comes out of someone's hide, who is prevented by nonmarket barriers such as nationality or discrimination from resisting an oppressor's appropriation of his or her slice of the pie. Profit is normally an indication of how well a person or an organization is serving the public and how much has been gained by productive activity to pass on to the future.... There are indeed higher and lower forms of profit, and the lower should serve and give way to the higher. The highest forms of profit are designated by the terms truth, beauty, and goodness.
                              FREDERICK TURNER, *Culture of Hope*, 230–31

In a crowded marketplace, aesthetics is often the only way to make a product stand out. Quality and price may be absolutes, but tastes still vary, and not every manufacturer has already learned how to make products that appeal to the senses.
                              VIRGINIA POSTREL, *The Substance of Style*, 2

"Eco" comes from the Greek word *oikos*, meaning home. Ecology is the study of home, while economics is the management of home. Ecologists attempt to define the conditions and principles that govern life's ability to flourish through time and change. Societies and our constructs, like economics, must adapt to those fundamentals defined by ecology. The challenge today is to put the "eco" back into economics and every aspect of our lives.
                              DAVID SUZUKI, *The Sacred Balance*, 8

This awakening of the inner mind will not be satisfied with personal expression alone. Its power will find its true fulfillment in returning the social arts of politics and economics to the folk. When this happens, politics will no longer be defined in the tired, pessimistic, and negatively senex manner as "the art of compromise" but as the *art of expression of the people's will and needs*. Politics will itself become the art of the people, the art of preserving and celebrating Mother Earth, the art of doing justice and keeping balance and harmony. Economics will become the *art of planetary management*, the art of living harmoniously within the necessary limits that the goods of the earth set for us, the art of common survival wherein all of creation and all its immense wealth—which is its health—is celebrated in balance and harmony. In this context, then, the arts of politics and economics can be expressions of shared reverence for our shared existence.
     MATTHEW FOX, *The Coming of the Cosmic Christ*, 201

Whatever strategies we try, we should endeavour to treat our working lives as experiments in the art of living.
     ROMAN KRZNARIC, *How Should We Live?*, 95

Many of the most exciting insights driving new economic thinking seem to be emerging from every quarter but economic departments themselves. There are of course some important exceptions to that, but they are too rare. So many of the transformative ideas are originating in other fields of thought such as psychology, architecture, sociology and complexity science. Economic theory would be wise to embrace what these other perspectives have to offer.
     KATE RAWORTH, *Doughnut Economics*, 244–45

One promising way of redefining the meaning of "economist" is to look at those who have gone beyond new economic thinking to new economic doing: the innovators who are evolving the economy one experiment at a time. Their impact is already reflected in the proven dynamism of the collaborative commons, in the vast potential of digital currencies and in the inspiring possibilities of regenerative design. As Donella Meadows made clear, the power of self-organization—the ability of system to add, change and evolve its own structure—is a high leverage point for whole

system change. And that unleashes a revolutionary thought: it makes economists of us all.
KATE RAWORTH, *Doughnut Economics*, 247–48

Ironically, however, Economic man—the ideal economic agent—is not free and responsible. He is possessed by one idea: his own material gain. He is a fanatic. He is selfishness incarnate. He must be so, in order to perform his economic function. Whenever standard economics faces a problem, it looks to economic man for the answer. The monomaniacal monster reveals what he would do in the circumstances. Most of the so-called laws of economics have been deduced from his consistently self-serving behavior.... These economic agents have been an organizing principle of standard economics.
GEORGE P. BROCKWAY, *The End of Economic Man*, 10

In the actual world, prices—including wages and interest rates—are set and accepted by human beings, not by axioms of rationality, nor by Adan Smith's "invisible hand," nor by the law of supply and demand nor by any other "law." This simple and obvious point makes it necessary to study economics as one of the "moral sciences," which consider the proper conduct of life.
GEORGE P. BROCKWAY, *The End of Economic Man*, 10

Political Science

Politics should be turned into art.
JOSEPH BEUYS, quoted in *Art Meets Science and Spirituality*, edited by Andreas Papadakis, Louwrien Wijers, and Johan Pijnappel, 9

The variety and perfection of the arts in Greece led thinkers to frame a generalized conception of art and to project the ideal of an art of organization of human activities as such—the arts of politics and morals.
JOHN DEWEY, *Art as Experience*, 25–6

The older tension in human affairs between conservative and liberal based on social orientation is being replaced with the tension between developers and ecologists based on orientation toward the natural world.

This new tension is becoming the primary tension in human affairs.... This new alignment should not be taken as if the ecology movement were a New Left or a new liberalism. For the ecology movement has moved the entire basis of the division into a new context. It is no longer a division based on political party or social class or ethnic group. It is division based on the human as one of the components within the larger community of the planet Earth.
THOMAS BERRY, *The Great Work*, 107

Beauty is the guide of politics, as it is the core of morality and speculative understanding.
FREDERICK TURNER, *Beauty: The Value of Values*, 35

[Our] biological nature is designed to exist within a cultural context that is in the broadest sense *classical*—by which I mean centered upon the values of truth, goodness, and beauty. Both the Right and the Left would disagree. The conservative Right regards human nature as essentially fallen, selfish, and individualistic.... The avant-garde Left, on the other hand, regards human nature as infinitely malleable, so that it can be easily "constructed" by society.
FREDERICK TURNER, *The Culture of Hope*, 7–8

The radical center sees art as the only place where the new concepts essential to real social progress can germinate and gestate. Current political struggles, where well-meaning people find themselves locked in bitter disagreement, are usually insoluble on their own terms. If negotiation or logic or the application of legal or moral rules could solve them, they would not be problems.
FREDERICK TURNER, *The Culture of Hope*, 10

The avant-garde [left] and the conservatives share certain metaphysical and philosophical assumptions, inherited from the nineteenth century, concretized in the polarization between Left and Right, and frozen in place by an esthetic and evaluative vocabulary that no longer corresponds to our best knowledge about the world. Those assumptions are the reason, not only for the ideological impasse, but also for many of the real problems of the contemporary arts, such as its desperate crisis of

originality, its failure to find an audience, and its isolation from vital intellectual currents in the human and natural sciences, religion, technology, and the environmental movement.
FREDERICK TURNER, *The Culture of Hope*, 4

What constitutes progress for the radical center is continuation of the natural evolution of the universe in a new, swifter, deeper way, through the cooperation of human beings with the rest of nature.
FREDERICK TURNER, *The Culture of Hope*, 11

Politics viewed as the serious effort to articulate excellence for society is itself a moral-aesthetic aspiration, and its achievements are properly deemed artworks that make claims to being both beautiful and good.
YI-FU TUAN, *Passing, Strange, and Wonderful*, 182

Anthropology

We must appreciate anew the universal necessity for art: why generally similar art forms have arisen in every culture, and why patterns of artistic development in cultures isolated from one another have followed similar courses.
ROBERT GRUDIN, *The Grace of Great Things*, 187

What does it mean that everywhere we find human beings seeking art in the same kind of designs and forms, from the Navajo Indians of North America to the natives of Africa to ancient Greece to the peasants of Europe? What is this thirst, the yearning in all peoples that cannot be denied?
ROLLO MAY, *My Quest for Beauty*, 227

We realize now that our common human language is not Esperanto or computers or something having to do with vocal cords and speech. It is, rather, our sense of proportion, our balance, harmony and other aspects of simple and fundamental form. Our universal language, in other words, is beauty. Beneath our loquacious chatter, there is a silent language of our whole being which yearns for art and the beauty from which art comes.

ROLLO MAY, *My Quest for Beauty*, 229

Fortunately there are also many instances of cultures that, either by luck or by foresight, have succeeded in creating a context in which flow is relatively easy to achieve. For instance, the pygmies of the Ituri forest described by Colin Turnbull live in harmony with one another and their environment, filling their lives with useful and challenging activities. When they are not hunting or improving their villages they sing, dance, play musical instruments, or tell stories to each other. As in many so-called "primitive" cultures, every adult in this pygmy society is expected to be a bit of an actor, singer, artist, and historian as well as a skilled worker.

MIHALY CSIKSZENTMIHALYI, *Flow*, 79–80

The basis of their [Loyalty Islanders] culture—and that is doubtless the significant fact for us—is artistic. Every one learned music, dancing, and song. Therefore it is natural for them to regard rhythm and grace in all the actions of life, and almost a matter of instinct to cultivate beauty in all social relationships.

HAVELOCK ELLIS, *The Dance of Life*, 13

The way in which tribal art, in its passionate spontaneity, is woven into the fabric of society is rooted in something that the modern world has lost, a cosmic confidence in ourselves and in the whole scheme of things. It is this confidence that enables tribal societies to resolve the conflicts and contradictions that are an inevitable part of life itself, to play with oppositions that would otherwise tear their worlds apart. Tribal art thus becomes a means of reconciling what is otherwise irreconcilable, of making the painful crises of life manageable—even of overcoming the ultimate disjunction, between life and death.

DAVID MAYBURY-LEWIS, *Millennium*, 163.

The arts by which primitive folk commemorated and transmitted their customs and institutions, arts that were communal, are the sources out of which all the fine arts have developed. The patterns that were

characteristic of weapons, rugs and blankets, baskets and jars, were marks of tribal union. Today the anthropologist relies upon the pattern carved on a club, or painted on a bowl to determine its origin. Rite and ceremony as well as legend bound the living and the dead in a common partnership.... Each of these communal modes of activity united the practical, the social, and educative in an integrated whole having esthetic form.
                          JOHN DEWEY, *Art as Experience*, 327

The appreciation of beauty on the part of primitive peoples, Mongolian, Indian, Arab, Egyptian, Greek, and Goth, was unerring. Because of this, their work is coming home to us today in another and truer Renaissance,... This Renaissance means a return to simple conventions in harmony with nature.
    FRANK LLOYD WRIGHT, Frank Lloyd Wright Collected Works, edited by Bruce Brooks Pfeiffer, 104–5

History

There is, however, something fundamental in humanity to which we shall always return because it is more or less immutable.... That is why a social historian has the right to set down an art of living, and to recall, beyond the prejudices and assumptions of his time, the needs of everlasting man.
                        ANDRE MAUROIX, *The Art of Living*, 10–11

Yet there is one realm where few have sought inspiration for our dilemmas about how to live: history. I believe that the future of the art of living can be found by gazing into the past. If we explore how people have lived in other epochs and cultures, we can draw out lessons for the challenges and opportunities of everyday life.
                        ROMAN KRZNARIC, *How Should We Live?*, ix–x

Our journey through history has revealed an array of possibilities, from finding beauty and spiritual meaning, to indulging our wild and feral selves; from satisfying our biophila and ecological unconscious, to living carbon-light so we can limit a warming world. We can be thankful there

is an internal harmony to all these approaches. They can be pursued without contradiction, and lead one to the other.
ROMAN KRZNARIC, *How Should We Live?* 215

[We] have changed the very chemistry of the planet, we have altered the biosystems, we have changed the topography and even the geological structure of the planet, structures and functions that have taken hundreds of millions and even billions of years to bring into existence. Such an order of change in its nature and in its order of magnitude has never before entered either into earth history or into human consciousness. These events, no less than the Fall of Rome, require a new historical vision to guide and inspire a new creative period not only in the human community, but also in the functioning of the earth itself, for our world is a world of historical realism.
THOMAS BERRY, *The Dream of the Earth*, xiii

We are born to a richer heritage, born to a higher level of that pedestal which the accumulation of knowledge and art raises as the ground and support of our being.... To those of us who study history not merely as a warning reminder of man's follies and crimes, but also as an encouraging remembrance of generative souls, the past ceases to be a depressing chamber of horrors; it becomes a celestial city, a spacious country of the mind, wherein a thousand saints, statesmen, inventors, scientists, poets, artists, musicians, lovers, and philosophers still live and speak, teach and carve and sing.
WILL AND ARIEL DURANT, *The Lessons of History*, 102

Geography

My own expectation is that the study of ecological geography will have a significant role to play in the future as one of the most effective disciplines leading to an integral human presence to the larger Earth community.
THOMAS BERRY, *The Great Work*, 98

The more attuned we are to the beauties of the world, the more we come to life and take joy in it. It is possible, then, to read the book as an orderly presentation of aesthetic experiences—a guide to the splendor of the earth and of the human creations on it. But I hope the book offers more. I see it as opening up a new view of culture and the aesthetic, such that the aesthetic is taken to be not merely a dimension or aspect of culture, but its emotional-aspirational core, both its drive and its goal.

YI-FU TUAN, *Passing Strange and Wonderful*, 1–2.

CONCLUSION: A THEORY OF THE ART OF LIVING

In theory, we can create beautiful lives by modifying our basic behavior with art, science, and religion seeking beauty, truth, and goodness. That sentence summarizes a general theory of the art of living as a way of life.

What are our most basic behavior? Like other animals, we create living space, obtain food, eat, court, have sex, parent, groom, play, build, form social bonds, flee, fight, and sleep. Those activities determine much that we experience in life.

What are our highest ideals? They include family, friendship, community, compassion, love, freedom, peace, and more. Beauty, truth, and goodness are especially significant. Seeking them can increase our experiences of other ideals. Our distant ancestors began seeking and celebrating those three ancient ideals thousands of years ago.

What do *beauty*, *truth*, and *goodness* mean? We call highly valued experiences *beautiful*. We describe qualities we experience as beautiful: harmony, radiance, wholeness, and others. *Truth* can mean knowledge of reality. *Goodness* can mean morality.

How can art, science, and religion lead to our highest ideals? Art can be a path toward beauty, science a path toward truth, and religion a path toward goodness. Each path can eventually lead toward all three. Art, science, and religion are primary sources of human civilization. We can become more civilized by cultivating our artistic, scientific, and religious inclinations.

How can everyone become artistic, scientific, and religious? We become artistic by refining a skill sufficiently. We become scientific by evaluating a theory rigorously and finding it adequately reliable or false. We become religious by devoting ourselves fully to an activity, idea, group, or interest, and/or by joining an organized religion.

What are everyday and specialized forms of art, science, and religion? Everyday forms modify our basic behavior. Everyone can learn them. The specialized forms are fine art (painting, sculpture, writing, singing, music, dance, theater, and more), social and natural science, and organized religion. Everyone can value those specialties and choose whether and how to participate in them.

What might happen if everyone sought our highest ideals through those everyday and specialized forms? Would we refine our behavior as well as possible? Would we heal conflicts that separate us as individuals and as nations? Would we create deep moral relationships with one another, with other species, and with nature? Would our skills in the art of living enable us to create beautiful lives? Would we create a science of the art of living? Let us seek answers to those questions.

What can go wrong? Art, science, and religion can become paths toward goals contrary to our ideals. For example, some people develop creative tactics in the art of war, use scientific knowledge to develop weapons of war, or feel religious enthusiasm for war. At their worst, art, science, and religion release our lowest human potential.

What is at stake? We live in times of unprecedented opportunity and unparalleled crisis. We may live at a turning point in history and need to make the right choices about how we live.

The primary biological and social reality of human life is that everyone is a member of the animal species *Homo sapiens*. In theory, by creating beautiful lives we can live in peace and harmony. We can reconcile the realism of our animal nature with the idealism of our highest human potential. The human species can become one human family at home on the earth and in the universe.

The earth and the universe are beautiful places. That is why we feel at home when we create beautiful lives. Let us fall in love with the world. Let us return home. We would all rejoice at that homecoming.

In theory, as we learn the art of living, we experience passion, compassion, empathy, sympathy, and other deep feelings. We learn to love one another, other species, and nature. Love is the emotional essence of a beautiful life, and the art of living is the art of loving.

Printed in the USA
CPSIA information can be obtained
at www.ICGtesting.com
LVHW021946060924
790343LV00033B/674